THE ENTERPRISE MODELLING AND STRATEGY PLANNING HANDBOOK

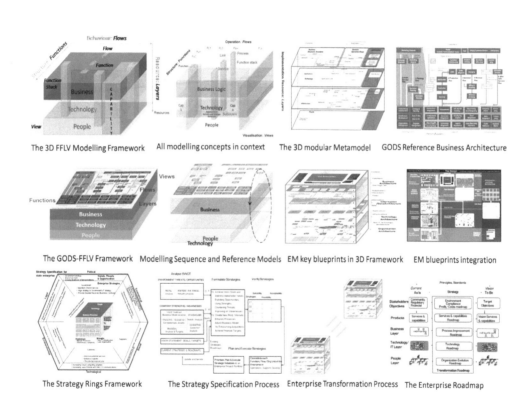

The 3D FFLV Modelling Framework   All modelling concepts in context   The 3D modular Metamodel   GODS Reference Business Architecture

The GODS-FFLV Framework   Modelling Sequence and Reference Models   EM key blueprints in 3D Framework   EM blueprints integration

The Strategy Rings Framework   The Strategy Specification Process   Enterprise Transformation Process   The Enterprise Roadmap

ADRIAN GRIGORIU

CONTENTS

ABOUT THE BOOK

The handbook is a concise and highly visual guide to the Enterprise and its Strategy Modelling.

The book aims to provide a unified end to end method that guides the enterprise designer, step by step, in modelling the enterprise structure, operation, information, organisation and strategy. It builds out a single integrated Enterprise Modelling development method out of new and the current diverging enterprise architecture and business modelling approaches of to today.

Since it supplies a set of A3 Posters that sum-up the key modelling aids, it may be used a reference manual, always at hand. The posters, once printed, could be employed as an aide memoire for the framework, templates, modelling and transformation process and the enterprise strategy design and mapping.

While the book describes an Enterprise wide Architecture modelling method, the activity is referred to as Enterprise Modelling to distinguish it from the Enterprise Architecture today which typically covers mainly IT.

The practitioner is the Enterprise Modeller, which is an Enterprise Architect that covers the whole enterprise. At times though, it is still called the Enterprise Architect or Designer.

The work covers though more than Enterprise Architecture in that it looks into all aspects of the enterprise. In focus though is still the IT technology which is the common denominator for all enterprises because it is deeply embedded in the enterprise operation today and it is core to its digital future.

The outcome of the Enterprise Modelling is the Enterprise Model (EM) which is the integrated set of the blueprints of various domains, each decomposable into further diagrams at the level of detail necessary in practice. The modelling approach reinstates the utility of such business concepts as Value Streams and Value Chains in the enterprise model context.

The handbook should be used as a practical guide to building own modelling approach by adapting the framework, generic business architecture and the various reference models supplied. The 2D/3D Design provided illustrates the integration of the proposed diagram types into the overall Enterprise Model.

It is the aim of this book to align the definitions of the key modelling elements of the enterprise, such as process, function, capability, service..., and their inter-relationships but also to put right such misinterpretations that Business Architecture is the same as Business Model or Business Capabilities map.

Newly in, are a System Design method, the logical build of a 3D modelling framework, the Capability modelling, the alignment of the Business Model to the Value Chain, the Strategy Circles design framework, the Posters, the evolution of the enterprise to digital...

The work is a continuation of the work already published and a synthesis of the work done in the field. It builds on the previous paradigms while it adds clarity and structure. The method exposed has its origins in both Business Theory (Value Chains, Value Streams, Business and Operating Models...) and Enterprise Architecture developments (Capabilities, IT Architecture...).

But, as always, there is still plenty of work to be done. This here second edition of the book adds section on the enterprise evolution to Digital and the Future Design of the Enterprise with Business Capabilities.

Why this book

The market is ripe for Enterprise Modelling. Companies are won over the utility of an overall Enterprise Model because it enables analysis and the strategic and operational alignment of the enterprise and renders it agile to rapid change. It also reduces the unnecessary complexity and its associated cost.

Still, there is reluctance to engage in modelling since the existing methods typically are reduced to IT and fail to deliver. The current approaches are fragmented, covering different aspects of the enterprise without providing the integrated view of the whole. There is no single standard in the Enterprise Architecture field. Moreover, most approaches have different definitions for every single concept or deliverable. There are also quite a few EA certification approaches that have their own and different training and criteria of accreditation. Large IT companies, business schools and consultancies have not provided direction either but contributed to the market fragmentation.

The reality is that each and every EA team has to build its own method, with various degrees of success, if any, before engaging in the enterprise architecture exercise. Because of that, most teams deliver the EA with results that vary wildly from case to case. As such, practices rather prefer to engage in mundane activities such as solution architectures, reviews, policing design developments... that do not deliver to the high expectations.

This step by step guide helps reduce this fragmentation by proposing one method while minimising the risks and costs of constructing own method time and again. It also guarantees results by increasing the predictability, repeatability, reliability and productivity of the Enterprise Modelling and Transformation effort.

The audience

Any Enterprise or Business Architecture team, in any industry and geography or EA consultancy would have an interest in the Enterprise Modelling Handbook since it will significantly reduce the cost and increase the productivity and predictability of their Enterprise Model development while guaranteeing results.

The audience consists as such of Business Designers, Business Enterprise and IT Architects, Business Model analysts, Business and Management Consultants indeed.

ENTERPRISE MODELLING ENABLES SOLUTIONS TO ENTERPRISE PROBLEM

The Enterprise Problem

An Enterprise is a group of people organised to deliver products employing technology.

The enterprise today suffers from

Organic Growth

from the rapid market growth and technology change executed in point solutions that duplicate existing functionality, increasing as such the complexity and cost of the enterprise

Silo Culture

from local tactical priorities which foster internal competition, poor collaboration and duplication in platforms, projects and technology

Temporary solutions turned permanent

because of the ever shortening time to market

Application patching

that in time inhibit the ability of the enterprise to implement business change and strategy

Lack of enterprise comprehension

- in the absence of a proper description of Enterprise operation

The Enterprise, as a result, is unnecessary complex, organized in silos and made of patched legacy with multiple and various point solutions that duplicate process, data, platforms and projects that increase cost, reduce reliability and deter change and, ultimately, the implementation of business strategy and objectives.

In the absence of an integrated enterprise model, there is no comprehensive big picture to enable the enterprise analysis, change and transformation. To remedy this we need to model the enterprise.

Modelling comes to enterprise rescue

Everyone in an enterprise has a diagram or at least a mental picture of how own part of the enterprise works. Yet diagrams and components often overlap in scope. Representations differ widely. There is, as such, no big picture that fuses the diagrams in a whole, there are many gaps, no navigability and no end to end blueprint. The diagrams are seldom discoverable since they are personal, stored in own drawers and PCs. In essence, these individual representations are disjoint, unreachable and, anyway, unable to paint the big picture of the enterprise.

The Enterprise Modelling remedies this by supplying the generic big picture and a framework that, once complied with, renders each individual diagram consistent in terms of components, I/O, representations and scope so that they all fit in the whole, the Enterprise Model, like parts in a car. But currently there is no such Modelling Framework. Hence, we cannot see the big picture and model its parts consistently.

Enterprise Modelling is the activity to describe the enterprise structure and operation in an overall blueprint. The Enterprise Model (EM) is a diagrammatical description of the enterprise. EM is represented as an integrated set of blueprints that illustrate the business organisation and flows of an enterprise and the technology and people resources that implement them. Information is part of the business entities, flows and, in general, of any entity of an enterprise.

The blueprints reuse the same components and representations, defined once, flow into each other without gaps and are stored and available from a virtual site. One can see own part at any level of detail, its place in the big picture and can navigate between the enterprise parts and from them to the implementing resources. Hence, one can understand a part in context, comprehend the enterprise end to end and analyse, fix and transform it.

We do model today almost any other system created by man. That is, we design it before we construct it. Not so with the enterprise which we built incrementally, with a minimum of upfront planning. But we can employ Enterprise Modelling to streamline and re-organise the enterprise. And then we can use EM to design enterprises like never before, when at best we had an entrepreneur's plan.

Enterprise Modelling versus Enterprise Architecture

Since the debates on a wider Enterprise Architecture (EA) that covers the whole enterprise have reached no conclusion so far, this book, rather than changing the scope of EA, tackles the issue of modelling the whole enterprise as Enterprise Modelling (EM). Typically, the current Enterprise Architecture efforts deliver only the IT sub-layer of the Enterprise Model. Enterprise Architecture (EA), as opposed to Enterprise Modelling, covers solely the Information Technology (IT).

The EM scope is the whole enterprise, the business and information architecture, people organisation and technology architecture.

While, in principle, EM and EA aim both to produce models, the EM concept permits us to explore the whole enterprise without the opposition and eternal debates of the existing IT EA camps.

Besides the EA function is hosted by IT and delivers to IT for IT, while the Enterprise Modelling function, to have visibility. should be located at the top of the enterprise in the CEO office or thereabouts. But without business and organisation views, EA has little meaning outside IT.

This book describes as such enterprise modelling, as opposed to enterprise IT modelling, even though it has its roots in EA and a good part of it refers to EA. Most previous EA work still applies though to Enterprise Modelling.

State of Enterprise Modelling and Architecture

Today, in the enterprise, there is no modelling practice but there are many models, architectures and diagrams designed by various people and units independently without any overarching conventions, principles and standards. Each establishes its own entities, naming conventions... The artefacts

- are not consistent in any respect
- overlap in boundaries and duplicate objects and connections
- do not interconnect
- describe unlike levels of detail
- serve only one stakeholder
- are designed with different tools
- are stored in various repositories

- are hard to find...

There is no framework today to fuse these individual partial blueprints in a single big picture. Hence, there is no synoptic view of the enterprise. There are though quite a few rather general modelling techniques for data, processes and software design such as IDEF, OO, BPMN... but, typically, they cover diagramming techniques rather than the way to model the enterprise out of the resulting artefacts. There are too many partial tools to model various aspects of the enterprise: Capability Maps, Value Chains, Value Networks, Business Models, Operating Models, Business Process Maps... Less known and newer are

- Service Blueprinting that enables the description of the service delivery to the customer
- Persona design is the personification of a customer segment in a generic person
- Customer Journey Mapping that illustrates the sequence of potential interactions of a persona with the enterprise from prospect to customer and after sales services
- User Interaction Design that, essentially, optimises the interaction with the customer

The Value of Enterprise Modelling

Enterprise Modelling may appear to be to most a long, expensive and potentially unrewarding development. Nonetheless, Enterprise Modelling returns benefits by enabling developments not possible without the overall blueprint of the enterprise.

The enterprise model documents the enterprise to enable understanding, analysis and further change. Enterprise Modelling, enables as such the flexibility and agility necessary to respond to market and regulatory changes. The model also facilitates the management of the ever growing complexity of the Enterprise.

In order to understand the enterprise structure and operation and be able to control its complexity, change and evolution, we need to model the enterprise.

The Enterprise Modelling enables:

The reduction of the Architecture Debt

By enforcing enterprise change and evolution according to agreed architecture and design principles.

Technical debt, in the enterprise architecture context, measures the departure of the current enterprise organization from the principles of enterprise architecture design. The more exceptions to the good rules of practice, the more the technical debt grows. Until the enterprise starts to falter.

The costs of debt will be ultimately reflected in the increased costs of maintenance, response time, reliability, agility, efficiency of new solutions design and ultimately, product costs and customer satisfaction.

If this debt is not repaid, that is corrected, "then it will keep on accumulating interest, making it hard to implement changes later on" (Wikipedia).

Most companies function with large technical debt because it means little to the business management compared to the focus on immediate business objectives and strategy. Hardest of all is to convince stakeholders to approve change and invest based solely on technical debt. Perhaps, because the technical debt is fully visible only to the enterprise architect.

But too often, the technical debt, is not considered in the building of the target enterprise state, based on the business goals alone, because the technical debt at the enterprise level, would be, unfortunately, of little concern to other audiences than architects.

The architect though, has to aim to reduce the technical debt during the strategy driven business transformation because it is unlikely that business would approve the transformation costs for the sake of the technical debt alone. A transformation of the enterprise would have to consider as such the reduction of the architecture debt. An enterprise restructuring must reduce the enterprise architecture debt. The debt represents the gap between the target state of the enterprise, dictated by the applying the architecture design principles, and the current state.

To prevent the accumulation of architecture debt all business and technical developments have to follow the enterprise architecture governance, principles, guidelines and roadmaps, process checkpoints and always effect change employing the enterprise model.

In particular, EM brings potential benefits to the Enterprise Operations, Governance, Evolution, Collaboration and Communications through:

Understanding of the enterprise and rapid fixes

of enterprise malfunctions and business change, the elimination of point solutions

Reduction in duplicate systems and silos

in organizations by documenting the enterprise structure and operation at all levels.

Portfolio based enterprise transformation

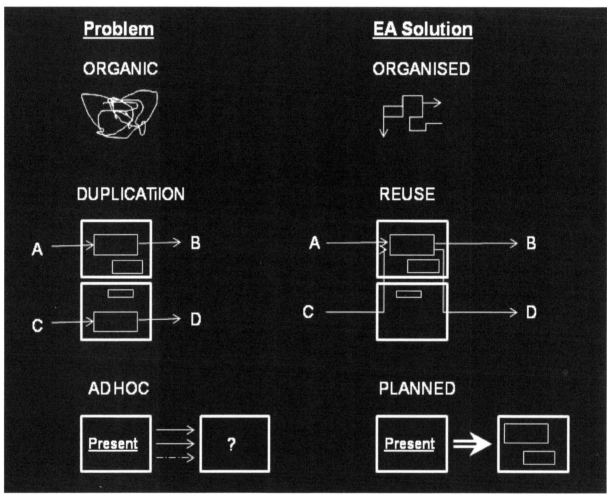

as opposed to ad hoc organic growth, that implements the business strategy by facilitating the mapping of the business strategy and by establishing architecture.

Alignment of technology and organization to business operation and objectives

Enables Long term investment planning

Facilitates Deployment of regulatory and such quality standards

such as SEI's Capability Maturity Model and Six Sigma and regulatory compliance frameworks such as SOX.

The Enterprise Modelling, like Strategy, is about long term thinking. It is the way an Enterprise can survive the furious rate of change and competition, the increasing acquisitions and outsourcing trends and the exponential increase in complexity and amount of information.

A model may also serve as a blueprint for building a new enterprise from scratch, even if the practice is not current today.

The EM, if kept current, is a reusable asset that continuously returns value to the enterprise. It is also an enterprise operation knowledge repository.

The EM enables the evolution towards the digital enterprise and IoT. It enables the nimbleness to counter the threats of entrants with new business models such as Sharing (Uber. Airbnb...).

Enterprise Modelling

Benefits for Enterprise Operations

- Identification and fixes of issues (defects, bottlenecks...)
- Integration of business functions, technology platforms...
- Improvement of processes
- Minimisation of duplication and unnecessary variation in platforms, technology
- Reuse
- Correlation of less joined up Enterprise level business activities such as BPM, Six/Lean Sigma, regulatory compliance...

Benefits for Enterprise Governance

- establishing standards, principles and guidelines for
- decision making
- change management
- investment

Benefits for Enterprise Evolution

- Agility from Lego like modularity, encapsulation, standardisation. architecture principles realisation
- Strategy planning and execution by covering all enterprise components, relationships
- Ease of planning of Outsourcing and Mergers & Acquisitions

Benefits for Enterprise Collaboration

since it establishes a common

- Understanding and vocabulary
- Big Picture and integrated enterprise wide set of blueprints
- Enterprise wide repository of systems information, artefacts, information...

Benefits for Enterprise Stakeholders

CEOs and Boards can

- Re-structure the Enterprise employing the enterprise model
- Inspect various aspects of the enterprise by browsing the Enterprise Model
- Improve the decision making process
- Analyse, direct and track Mergers & Acquisitions

Line-Of-Business executives

- Improve operation and investments inside and between departments
- Model and measure performance

- o Manage assets and inventories generated and stored by the EM tool

CTO, CIO and Chief IT Architects

- o Transform business strategy into technology, applications and infrastructure planning
- o Add simplification, modularization and optimization measures in strategy planning

Business and Technology Strategists

- o build (according to the method provided) and trace strategy to the Enterprise business functions, technology and organisation
- o measure progress of strategy implementation

Architects and Quality Engineers

- o set enterprise wide architecture guidelines and technology selection standards
- o release common data vocabulary and methodology for the Enterprise
- o align domain blueprints

Program Managers

- o may adopt a holistic Program Portfolio approach that makes possible the understanding of dependencies, realization of synergies and ultimately, the strategy execution

Regulatory bodies

- o do position compliance (SOX, Basel X, ...) controls in the enterprise business architecture

The enterprise as a whole can be improved through:

Streamlining

operations simplification by reducing duplication and minimising unjustified variety in products, platforms, projects... in line with the architecture principles

Alignment

of technology operation and people roles and organisation to real business processes, all layers of the enterprise wide model

Agility

through modularity and change without side effects that enable quick adaptation to industry, regulatory and market moves.

Strategic planning

- taking into consideration both enterprise wide processes and resources

In an enterprise, for instance, the Business Process Management (BPM) activity that describes the business flows is usually performed independently of the architecture effort. Since that usually means the modelling of the flows as lists of activities, without pinpointing where and by whom/what the processes are executed, BPM, taken in isolation, is hardly delivering value in practice. But equally, an architecture, without being driven by and validated against flows, may be flawed, because it may not implement properly the flows that return value to stakeholders.

Typically, the architecture illustrates the structure of a system, like the anatomy of a body shows parts or nodes in interconnections. The operation of a system, consisting of the system flows, is like the physiology of a live body. It realises the mission of the system. But, while a very important part of the design, the signals/flows are not typically exhibited with the architecture that describes only the resulting structure. The system flows though determine and validate the nodes and connections structure.

SYSTEM MODELLING 101, THE SYSTEM MODELLING POSTER

An Enterprise is a System which, according to the Business Dictionary, is "*an organized, purposeful structure that consists of interrelated and interdependent elements*". Since the enterprise is a system, it can be modelled using a similar approach. Hence, it is good to understand how a system is modelled before turning to the enterprise.

A system, as a real life object, can be represented as a three dimensional body which contains all its parts, nodes, interconnections, signals, information... all implemented by various technologies. The cube representation can be logically sectioned, scanned, rotated... for inspection and analysis.

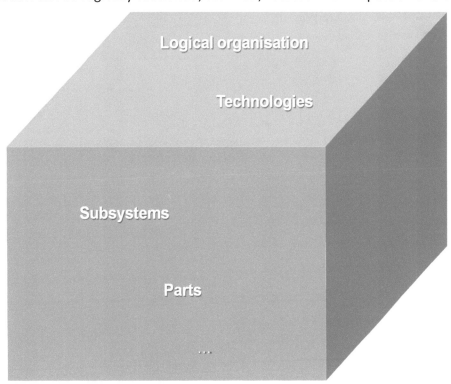

The architecture of a system is, essentially, its static structure consisting of the system nodes or functions in interconnections. In practice though, the architecture denotes, more often than not, the schematics of a system, its graphical description consisting of a set of linked diagrams, each illustrating, at various levels of detail, the system nodes (functions) in interconnections.

The dynamic behaviour of a system is described by signals flowing over its nodes and connections. While not explicitly represented in architecture, it is the key part of the system design from which the nodes structure and interconnections result.

Similarly, a car schematics describes the sub-system and parts in interconnection that enable the car fuel, air, electricity... flows. Any system can be logically described by its structure (nodes in interconnections) and its signals flow. But both Nodes and Signals are implemented in one or more technologies at various layers. Any component of a system is part of a Node, Signal and an implementation Layer.

A three-Dimensional System/Enterprise Modelling Framework

Since any system can essentially be described by its Structure (Nodes or Functions in interconnection), Behaviour or Operation (Signal or Flows) and physical Resource Layers, it can be indeed represented as a three dimensional body such as a cube, as assumed previously.

A system can be described by its Logic and Implementation. The abstract logic, consisting of the system structure and behaviour, is executed by the physical implementation. The structure of a TV set or PC is described by a block diagram, its behaviour or operation is illustrated by signals paths through a sequence of nodes, while both are realised in a particular technology.

While the implementation depends on the technology generation, the system logic (block diagram and signal flows) remains essentially the same.

Any system is described as such by its

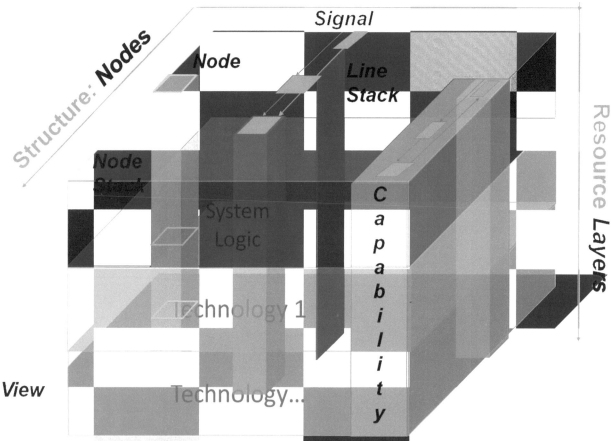

- system Logic consisting of the
  - o system context and interactions
  - o static Structure, i.e. nodes/functions interconnected by links, expressed in block diagrams.
  - o dynamic Behaviour, the flow of parts/paper/docs/signals/messages... over links between nodes/functions expressed, typically, in object, sequence or swimlane diagrams

- o system data map
- physical Resources, that implement the abstract functions and flows, grouped in layers
- The state of a node is specified in a state diagram showing the states a node passes through and the events that move the node from one state to another.
- Block and swimlane diagrams at the logic layer map at the implementation layers onto the physical resources that execute them.
- Information and parts are processed and stored in functions and are transported between functions over links.

A Node Stack or a Line Stack denote the abstract node plus the resources that implement it, called as such because they expand over a few layers and are represented as a top down column in the picture. To avoid clutter the line stacks are not shown in many subsequent representations. But, the issue must be noted because EA tools are not designed to describe a connection stack from flow to wire or transportation band...

Any point in the three dimensional space would belong to a node, a flow and a layer at the same time. Any system diagram as such would illustrate at least a Function in a Flow at either a logical or implementation layer.

To fit in the overall integrated architecture, any blueprint shall consist of a subset of the same set of components. The component types and their relationships should be defined only once in the metamodel which exists for this very purpose. The metamodel is usually illustrated as an entity relationship or class diagram. Other elements of an architecture such as, Interfaces, Information, Rules... would also be described in the metamodel. The metamodel is in fact, the model of the system model or the architecture of the system architecture.

All component and link types in a system model should be described as such in the metamodel. At the same time, all components and links, which instantiate the types described in the metamodel, should be stored in a model repository so that they can be reused by all diagrams. The metamodel is, in fact, the DB schema of this component database or repository.

To recap, any component and link in the architecture repository should be of a class or type defined in the metamodel and should support the relationships defined in there.

For a consistent look and feel, the same modelling symbols should be used, rather than having them reinvented for each model.

The three-Dimensional System Modelling Framework describes the three dimensional structure of either a system or an enterprise architecture:

1st Dimension: Nodes (Functions for the enterprise) and Links (representing Structure)

2nd Dimension Signals (Flows for the enterprise) (illustrating the dynamic Operation)

3rd Dimension: the Physical Resources in Implementation Layers

such as people and technology sub-layers separated on types of technology.

Any component of a diagram is represented as such as a point in this 3D space with coordinates denoting a Function or Link of a Flow belonging to a Layer.

Views help visualise a system. A View exhibits only that aspect of the enterprise of interest to us since it filters out all the non-relevant information. A view may consist of one or more related diagrams and looks like a two (or three) dimensional section through the system cube, same as a scan through a human body.

The modelling outcome is the system model or architecture which is the description of the system.

The blueprints components are aligned:

- Vertically; the node or link stack (not shown in the picture for clarity) align the system logic elements to the implementing physical technology
- Laterally, links that end on one blueprint continue on another
- Zoom-in/out; any node and link can be decomposed in further detail to subsequent blueprints; the entire navigation is done at the new level of detail

The proposed modelling framework defines this 3D structure and the metamodel which determines the components of a model.

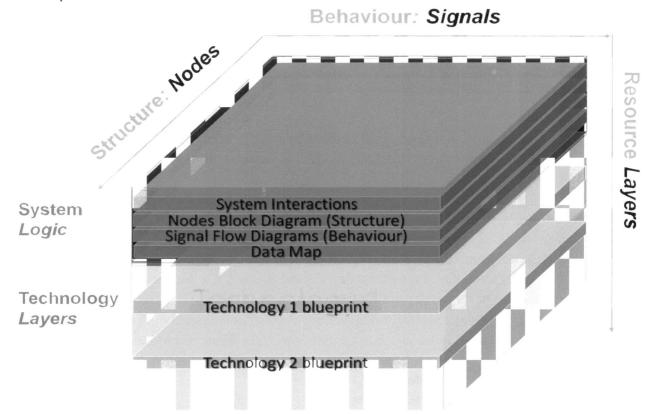

An extended framework also describes the architecture patterns, templates, principles, decomposition, graphical navigation of the model and the architecture modelling process.

The modelling framework offers consistency, predictability, repeatability in results while minimises the amount of work necessary and as such the costs of developments and the efforts to "re-invent the wheel".

But the job of an Architect is not really to re-invent the framework, as too often occurs today, but to customise and populate the framework with the information specific to own system.

Modelling a system by analogy with the anatomy and physiology of the human body

Perhaps, the human body is one of the first systems that people attempted to model so that they can understand it, cure and repair it. In short, the human anatomy describes the structure of the body while the physiology illustrates its behaviour or operation.

The description of a system, and as such of an enterprise, could, to a large degree, be done by analogy with the anatomy and physiology of the human body.

Here (http://www.healthline.com/human-body-maps) is an example of modelling and visualisation of the body in 2D/3D. The body vital systems are comparable to system capabilities; body organs to functions (nodes or blocks) and body flows to system flows.

Menu choices select views displaying various body aspects: capabilities, functions, flows. Or, on the representation, one can click to select a form, that will be displayed in a new window, and then inspect, section and rotate it.

A system or enterprise components comparison to the body parts:

- **A Capability**: an ability of a system to do and deliver something of value to someone. It consists of and is described by all blocks and processes that implement it. By comparison, a body has the vital processes, the capability to breath to oxygenate the body, to feed and digest in order to fuel the body, to feel to be able to react to the outer world, to think to fight another day... A system/enterprise Capability consists of all Functions, Links and Flows that implement it. Take for instance, the capability to manufacture a product. A capability is represented as an Enterprise View

- **A Function** compares to a body organ (ex: heart); it is a node or block in a system model

- **A Flow**: a body flow, such as the oxygenated blood journey through the arterial system and organs. While a body flow represents a sequence of body actions performed in organs linked by arteries, a system or enterprise flow is a sequence of activities executed by interconnected functions. For an enterprise, "From invoice to cash" is a flow.

- **A Line**: a link between functions very much like an artery or nerve that interconnects organs and body parts. In the Enterprise, lines are manual, transportation bands or network connections.

- **A View**: representing a cross-section through the Enterprise compares to a specific aspect of a body (the arteries of the circulatory system) same as a virtual cut or a CT (Computer Tomography) body scan. A View represents not a specific part/function but a visualisation technique that filters only an aspect of interest to an analysis.

- **Information** in a system, as in the Enterprise, is stored in various nodes; the information in human body lies in cells, DNA, in memory...

- A **Map** is a representation of a number of blocks on a sheet.

The body interaction with the environment for eating, breathing, sensing... Is similar in the Enterprise to the interaction with the environment and external stakeholders, described in Use Case Scenarios.

A doctor, a surgeon cannot diagnose or operate without being familiar with all body organs, systems and vital processes, their anatomy (structure) and physiology (operation). Similarly, an Enterprise Modeller cannot diagnose without knowledge of all business Functions, Flows and the resources that implement them. Even more, doctors specialize in one of these systems like architects do in the Enterprise.

System Modelling, step by step

This is the system design approach used throughout the enterprise modelling process.

To design a system from scratch one has to:

SM -1 analyse and document interaction flows

employing Use Cases (UC). Every UC identifies a system capability

For each Use Case (Capability) document

SM -2 document all Scenarios, using UML

SM -3 group Scenario activities in Nodes and illustrate them in a block diagram

SM -4 illustrate Scenarios over Nodes in Sequence/Swimlane/Object diagrams

SM -5 illustrate in State diagrams the transitions between states of nodes

and the events that cause them

SM -6 *identify nods, interfaces and shared links(lines) by looking at each scenario*

SM -7 *identify Information inside Functions, Decision points and Rules*
that determine subsequent action parameters and branching

SM -8 *group nodes and links*
when employed by more capabilities to reduce duplication

SM -9 *iterate modelling to refine nodes, Interfaces, links...*

> **Nodes boundaries and Interfaces**
>
> **Permanent Links between Nodes**
>
> **Information/Rules in Nodes**
>
> **Add new Capabilities, Nodes, Flows, Information, Rules, Interfaces**
>
> **Add new stakeholders scenarios**

SM -10 *select, if system designed from scratch, or otheriwise document tech. for each nod, link*

A capability is a sub-system in terms of its Functions, Flows and Resources. Each capability, implementing a Use Case of the system, can be described by a block and flow diagram and by its Information map, decision rules, interfaces and access protocols.

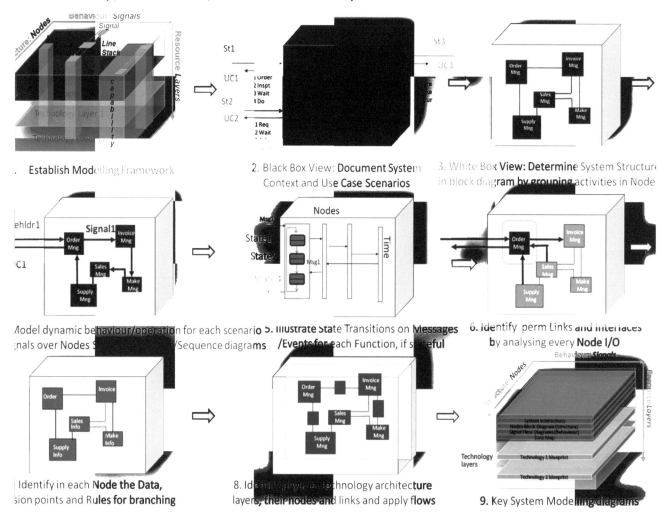

A node/function or link may serve more capabilities. Thus, capabilities are in practice not independent/orthogonal. To sum up, a system is composed of and described by its capabilities. Since any system consists of a number of capabilities, and a capability can be described as a subsystem in terms of its Functions, Flows and Resources, the system can be represented by the integrated blueprint of its capabilities.

Each capability, implementing a Use Case of the system, can be described, as above, by a block and flow diagram and by its Information map, decision rules, interfaces and access protocols. To reduce duplication, a node/function or link may serve more capabilities. Thus, capabilities are not totallyindependent, orthogonal. The key system capabilities may be identified by stakeholder Use Cases.

As a corollary, the system strategy and requirements can be easily mapped by customers (or business) to capabilities and by the architects to the components of capabilities for implementation,ensuring as such, the cascade of high level requirements from top to bottom.

ENTERPRISE MODELLING FRAMEWORK, GODS-FFLV, THE FRAMEWORK POSTER

The modelling framework describes the structure of the system/enterprise Model, that is, the spatial organisation of its key dimensions. It illustrates, for all audiences, how various blueprints fit into the whole model. All system/enterprise blueprints should have the same structure i.e. components as the dimensions of the framework. The modelling framework is the chassis on which any system Model can be built, repeatedly and consistently, from parts developed independently that conform to the framework.

The Metamodel illustrates all the Enterprise Model (EM) components types and their implicit relationships, in addition to the Framework components. For instance, any node/function in the business layer would be always linked to/implemented by a node/application in a technology platform and/or a role in the people organisation layer.

To fit in the whole, any stakeholder blueprint shall consist of the same types of components in the same relationship as in the metamodel. For this reason, the metamodel types and relationships should be implemented in the modelling tool repository database schema.

All objects in the repository would be the entities of the enterprise and the components of the Enterprise Model.

The metamodel complements the EM framework. But while the metamodel, expressed in an entity relationship/class diagram, addresses the designer, the EM framework addresses the general user audience, since it illustrates graphically the structure in which the various enterprise blueprints fit to form the overall Enterprise Model.

The EM Framework graphical representation could be used as the basis for the Graphical User Interface for the Enterprise Model navigation.

An extended framework also describes the Enterprise Model patterns, decomposition and navigation and the architectural design principles and standards.

Modelling your Business with a generic Business Architecture, GODS

Enter GODS, a proposed Value Chain and generic logical partitioning of the Enterprise based on the observation that any enterprise has Governance, Operations, Development and enterprise Support (GODS) Functions.

GODS is rooted in Michael Porter's Value Chain from which it further splits the newly defined Enterprise Governance and Development functions.

The enterprise Governance and Development functions are newly introduced in this model since they do not exist in Porter's Value Chain. The GODS Operations function represents essentially the Porter's Primary set of activities rather updated to include Marketing Research and the subsequent Product

Planning while Marketing in Porters looks more like advertising. Porter's Support activities are essentially the same as GODS enterprise Support.

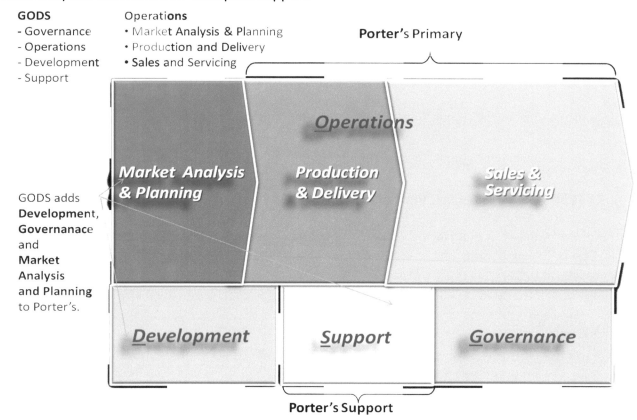

The enterprise Value Chain is essentially the activity flow that delivers the Product, the key deliverable of the enterprise, to the customer. The Value Chain is as such the product delivery Capability of the enterprise. It is also the main Use Case for the enterprise.

The Value Chain consists of links which are, in turn, capabilities in themselves that deliver into the Value Chain. Hence, a Value Chain consists essentially of a chain of Capabilities.

There are the internal enterprise capabilities (not visible to external stakeholders) that deliver value into and support other capabilities or stakeholders

GODS consists, in fact, of the Governance, Operations value chain, Development and Support Capabilities of the enterprise. These top level capabilities can be further decomposed.

The Value Chain and GODS, mapped onto each other, show that the GODS Support and Development capabilities may map on Porter's Support, GODS Operations on Porter's Primary and GODS Governance is entirely new.

Here is an extended GODS build on Capabilities nominated at the top of the picture: Market & Plan, Produce & Deliver, Sell & Service and the enterprise Development, Support and Governance.

The customer, the main stakeholder of the enterprise, beside the owner, the employee, the enterprise itself and the environment/community has quite a few interactions with the enterprise beginning with the prospective customer till the time it employs the enterprise after sales services.

Hence, the GODS one page generic business architecture that consists of the following capabilities:

.1. *The Market Research and Plan Capabilities consisting of*

Marketing research capability assesses the Demand Flow that investigates market demand

Business planning capability over the Planning Flow that delivers into the Production capability

.2. *The Produce and Deliver Capabilities made of the following SCOR like Flow*

Source

Make (Production)

Deliver (Distribution)

.3. The Sell and Service capabilities consisting of the

Sales capability delivered by a Demand Flow value stream

Order Management capability

Service capability around the After Sales Flow

Revenue accrual capability around the Revenue Flows

Provisioning/Subscription

To this the enterprise Governance, Development and Support capabilities must be added.

The GODS One Page Generic Business Architecture

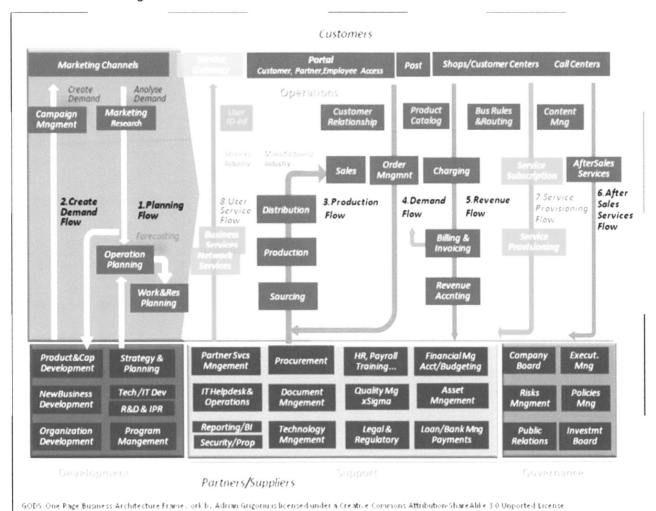

GODS One Page Business Architecture Framework by Adrian Grigoriu is licensed under a Creative Commons Attribution-ShareAlike 3.0 Unported License

It is used for wide communications and presentation of Enterprise operation. It is a reference framework for integration of solutions architectures. The one page overall enterprise model consists, in fact, of an one page for each layer: applications, infrastructure, non-IT technology people organisation.

In the architecture diagram a line is an information/material/ control flow. An arrow at the end of a line shows the destination of the flow. Typically the one page architecture refers to the Operations Architecture that delivers the product. In addition to the Operations model there should be one pages for Support, Development and Governance.

GODS Functions alignment to the Value Chain

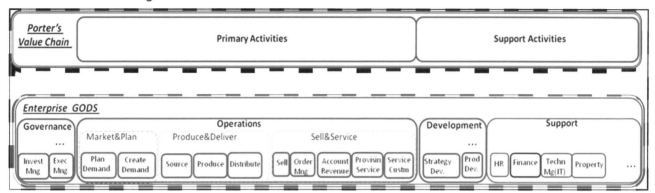

The Enterprise Modelling Framework, FFLV: Functions-Flows-Layers-Views

An enterprise, as any body in nature or man made system, can be described in three dimensions. Any system can be completely described by its logical Structure and Behaviour and the physical Resources that implement them.

A System Architecture (SA) consists and is described by its logical structure (nodes and links), behaviour (flows) and the physical resources that implement them. Thus, a System Architecture has three dimensions: structure in nodes, behaviour in flows, implementations resources and as such can be represented as a three dimensional body, a cube for instance.

- Structure, the static view of a system, consists of interconnected nodes.
- Behaviour/Operation, the dynamic aspect of the system, is composed of Flows. A Flow consists of an end to end (e2e) process executed across nodes, in sequence.
- Physical resources, such as material, technology..., implement Structure (nodes) and Behaviour (flows) which are abstract.

The Physical implementation can be depicted by resources grouped in layers of the same type.

Since the enterprise is a system, any enterprise can be described by its structure, operation (behaviour) and the resources that implement them.

Thus, an Enterprise Model (EM) consists and is described by its Nodes or Functions (structure), Flow (operation) and the People and Technology (resource layers) that implement them.

An Enterprise Model (EM) is represented as such in three dimensions as a cube or parallelepiped.

The system logic is implemented and illustrated by its structure (nodes and links) and behaviour (flows). It can be illustrated, in a single page, as a block diagram of the key flows over nodes.

The Business Architecture (BA) is by definition the enterprise logic. It is implemented and illustrated by the structure and operation of the enterprise. The Business Architecture can be depicted in a single page in block diagram of the key flows over nodes.

The Technology and People resources can be organised in physical layers that consist of sub-layers... Ex: IT Technology consists of the Applications, Servers, Storage, Networks... sub-layers. The Business Architecture is the first layer of the Enterprise Model that shapes the other layers.

The three dimensions of the Framework and System Model

  X : Nodes/Functions and connections, illustrating the Structure

  Y : Flows over Functions describing the Operation (Behaviour) of the system

  Z : Resources physically implementing logical nodes and flows grouped on types in layers

A three dimensional cube model can be used to describe any system in terms of static structure, dynamic behaviour and implementation layers of technology. The cube representation also illustrates the key business concepts of Process, Service and Capabilities in each others' context.

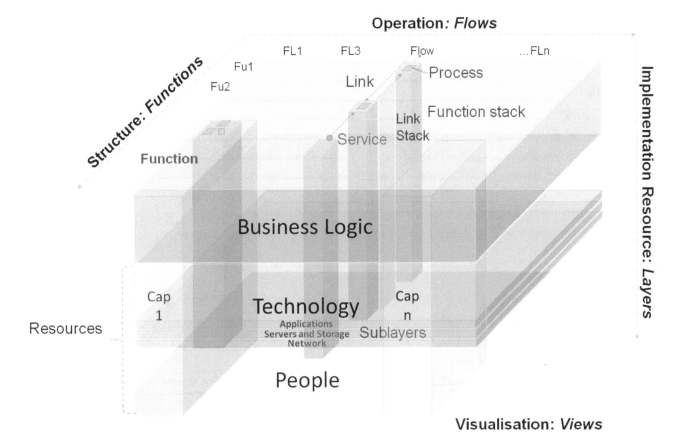

Concepts Definition: Function, Flow, Capability, Service...

The representation of the enterprise modelling exposes in context the concepts of

Process

is an activity, a basic element of the EA

Functions

are clusters of related functionality in which the enterprise is logically partitioned. A Function groups

- Processes of a similar kind
- Information which is hold in storage and transformed by processes in Function
- Rules that guide the process execution
- Interfaces to other processes, to people and technology

Function/Line Stack

A Function/Line and its afferent resources, i.e. the Technology and People roles that implement the it. A stack is visualised as a cross-section through all layers of the enterprise cube.

Flows

Flows or value streams are workflows executed, end to end, in and across Functions to deliver products, services and in general value to stakeholders. They describe the enterprise operation, the enterprise dynamic/behavioural aspects.

A Logical flow consists of an outcome, a product (part, information...) that is transmitted over a Line/Link. A Flow is implemented over nodes in interconnections implemented at resource layers.

Layers

are abstract strata in the enterprise describing the logical operation, technology an people resources. They consist of an unlimited number of sub-layers. They are called layer because they look like horizontal slices through the framework cube, as illustrated.

Views

are filters or cross-sections in the Enterprise body. The Enterprise, seen through the eyes of a stakeholder, is solely a View reflecting own work concerns. The Enterprise is ultimately described by the integrated systems of all Views.

Capability

an operation an enterprise performs that delivers an outcome to a stakeholder. The capability consists of Functions, Flows and the related People & Technology that execute it. Hence, any capability can be described by this same cube structure. A capability is illustrated as an enterprise View consisting of several Functions, Flows and resources rather than a single structural element, i.e. a node or Function, which is too often the assumption. But a capability, can be implemented by at least a node/Function. Following this assumption Capabilities and Functions are, at high level, interchangeable in the following pages.

Service

In the restricted sense, it is an encapsulated Capability accessed through a formal interface, and consists of the Functions, Flows and resources that deliver the service.

The Nodes and Lines, while are the ubiquitous elements of all layers, are realised in various ways, as in the picture.

The Architectural entities, Nodes and Links, in each enterprise layer

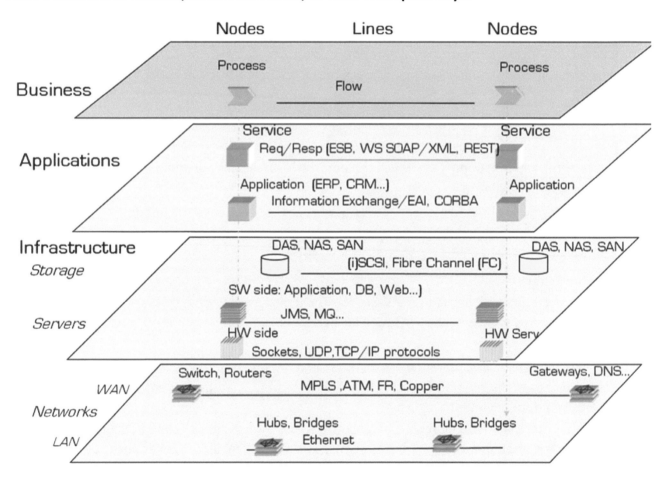

Use patterns to map the Functions and Flows in the Business logic layer to Nodes and Lines in lower layers.

- at the Business logic layer there are

28

- o Functions and Flows
- ▪ at Applications layer nodes and lines are
  - o Applications components and Information exchanges
  - o Web services - Request/Response
- ▪ at Infrastructure layer

  Storage sub-layer,
  - o Storage Areas (DAS, NAS...) - Channels

  Server layer
  - o SW sub-layer: Containers, DB - messaging buses;
  - o HW sub-layer: Servers - Sockets, TCP, UDP/IP protocols

  Network layer
  - o WAN: Switches, Routers, DNSs - MPLS, ATM, FR...
  - o LAN: Hubs, Bridges - Ethernet links

No other technology is illustrated but most technologies would have processing Nodes and transmission Links.

Any Line, as well as Node, illustrated in the business logic layer, is implemented at resources layers by either technology or/and people. Hence one can navigate a Flow to discover what implements it, as for instance, UDP/IP/Ethernet links or a production band or simply human couriers. Most tools do not allow Links as full objects of the inventory, unfortunately which is a major impediment in designing a complete enterprise model.

Hierarchical Model Decomposition

The Enterprise/Capability model decomposition is done on any of the three axis: Functions, Flows and Resource Layers. Any capability is decomposed like the enterprise model as a hierarchy of Functions, Flows or Technology and People organization. This is useful for the hierarchy of detail blueprints.

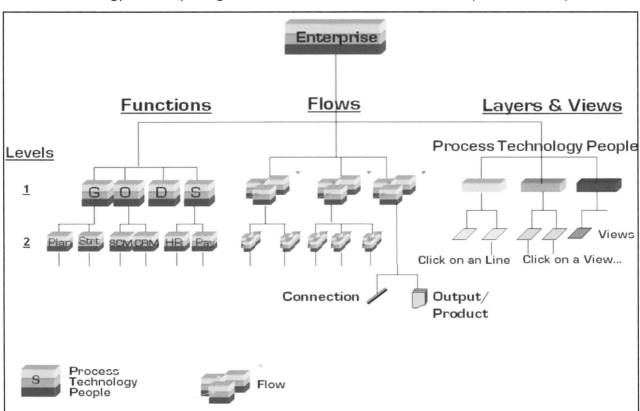

The Enterprise Modelling Metamodel

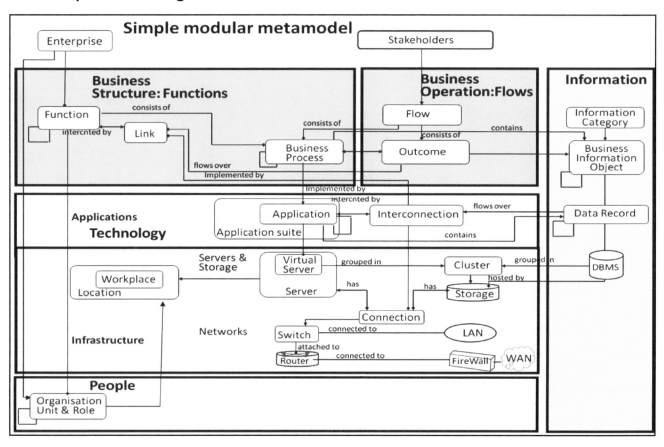

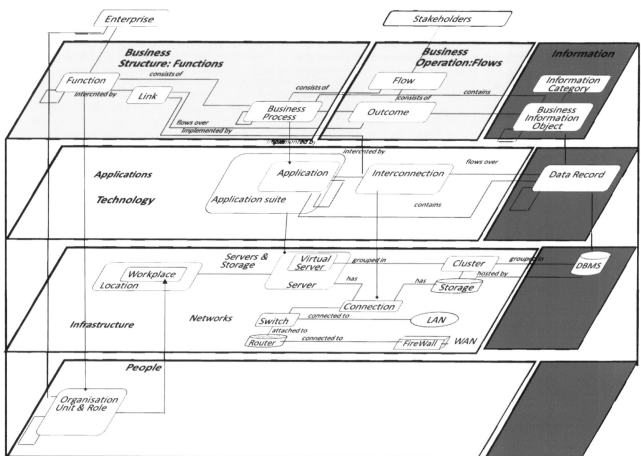

The metamodel is illustrating in an entity-relationship (class) diagram the enterprise model key components and their relationships to each other. It must be established upfront to support the definition of the diagrams component types and the relationships between them.

Each layer has own metamodel. The Enterprise Model metamodel is modular, composed of the linked metamodels of each layer: Process, Technology and People.

The key elements of the overall metamodel are the Functions, Flows, Systems, Links, Information asset, Data element and People roles. Interfaces, Rules... must be added.

The Business Architecture is described by the Business Structure and Business Behaviour metamodels that share the Process element. The Technology metamodel only shows IT and it is partitioned in Applications and Infrastructure sub-layers. Other technology sub-layers could be added.

The Information metamodel, set on the right side, links to all other layer metamodels.

Strategy, roadmapping metamodels could be added, when needed. A class diagram showing entities such as Vision, Goals linked to capabilities would express the Strategy or "Motivation" metamodel. Still, in the work here, a simple strategic planning diagram showing interactions between these elements is preferred to avoid entity relationship or class diagrams with which many business readers are unfamiliar. The metamodel represents the entity relationship or class diagram for the EM repository design that should be embedded in the tool database.

Key diagrams of any Enterprise, capability or solution Architecture

Both the enterprise and a capability can be described by this same set of key blueprints as in the

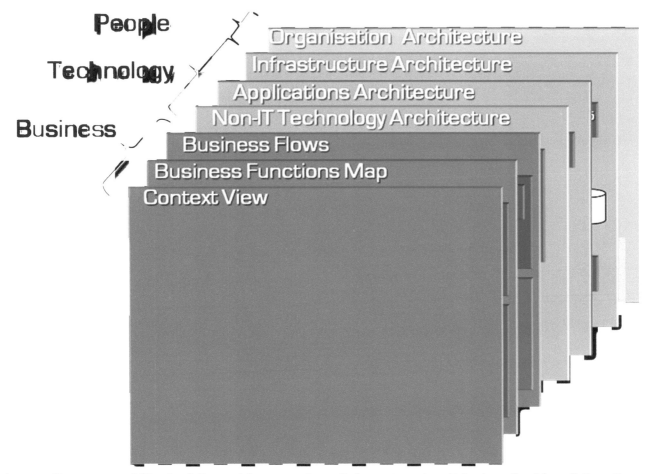

picture. Since a capability is delivered by a section of the enterprise, it is described by all Functions, Flows, Information and the Technology and People roles that implement it. It is illustrated by the same set and type of diagrams the enterprise model is: Business Architecture (Context and Stakeholders,

Business Functions Map (structure), Business Flows (Behaviour)), Technology (non-IT Technology Architecture, Applications, Infrastructure... Architectures), People Organisation.

Enterprise Modelling Framework in a picture, GODS-FFLV

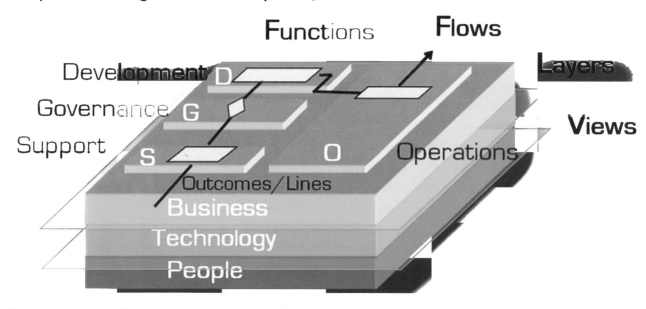

The Navigation of FFLV Enterprise Model on Menus and Click on Entity

It enables the modeller to implement navigation of the EM on the web site and/or in a modelling tool.

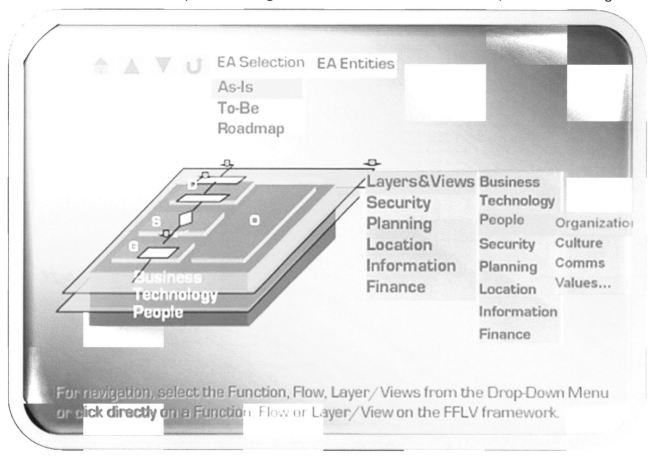

The model can be browsed, as shown in pictures from menu bars and/or by clicking on various elements. You can choose a Capability (not shown except as G-O-D-S), a Function from the menu or diagram, a Flow, a Layer... You can move from process or information to the technology that sustains it or the people that execute it.

A capability view can be added in the Menus. A capability can be navigated from the menu bars or

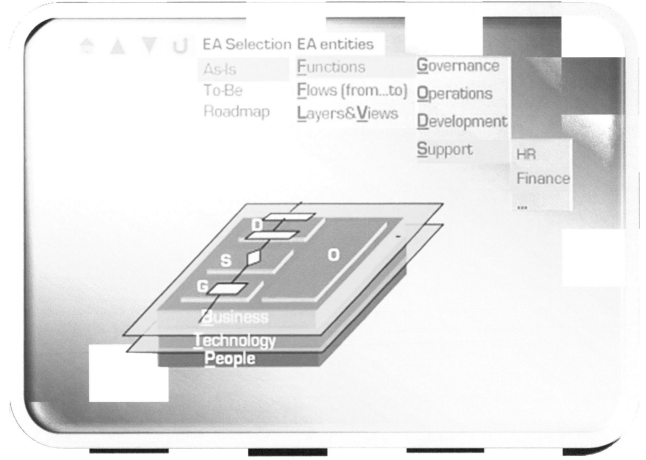

clicking on its components as in pictures.

Architecture principles

The Architecture Principles and Technology Standards are an essential part of the framework in the design of the Target EM. They shape the As-Is transformation into the To-Be Enterprise.

The technology standards guide the technology roadmapping which guide the technology change, selection and replacement. An obsolescence systems and technology roadmap is also a must to address technology change.

Decoupling/Modularization

▪ Design modular functions on the principle of minimal coupling and maximal internal cohesion.

Encapsulation

Define access to modules through interfaces to limit random access to internals and to hide implementation technology

Layering

Design architectural layers, coherent enterprise wide grouping of components, so that a layer always provides services to other layers (above) through defined interfaces.

Hierarchical design

Provide a system decomposition tree to insulate designers from unnecessary detail.

Distribution agnostic

Nodes and services should be designed with transparent distribution in mind so that they can be relocated.

Standardization

Discover patterns and standardize components, interfaces, processes.

Reuse and reduce duplication

A system function shall be specified only once as a single service and then reused to minimize duplication in functions, processes, data and platforms.

Design employing services paradigm

Use services, service bus pattern and technology for application integration.

Design Standards

Employ Containers/Application hosting technology

Since they provide of the shelf horizontal services as transparent distribution, security, access to databases etc.

Virtualise technology

Introduce interfaces, a layer between the access and implementation technology, to abstract the technology and its entities such as servers, connections. Deploy virtualization for servers, storage, storage, I/O, networks, application and desktops.

Use technology Appliances

Use Off-the-Shelf appliances (firewalls, proxies, gateways…) like chips in the hardware industry.

Converge media networks

to replace current two or more separate networks into one.

Reuse, Buy or Build in this order

SETUP ENTERPRISE MODELLING FUNCTION

EM Setup -1 Establish the Drivers for Enterprise Modelling

- An imminent business transformation
- An imminent Merger or Acquisition (M&A)
- A decision to outsource business functions
- Adoption of a Cloud strategy
- A requirement to implement regulatory changes
- A business process improvement initiative
- A company re-organization
- Adoption of new business models
- An upgrade of obsolete key technology
- Establishment of a new company
- Conscient decision to better the enterprise

EM Setup -2 Define Mission, Assess and get Business Case for Enterprise Modelling Approved

In the long term, by employing EM and transforming the enterprise according to architecture principles, the enterprise turns more efficient from streamlining, process improvement, technology alignment to business operation... while costs go down from reduced duplication and complexity, in general.

The Business Case is relative to the business as usual case, that is, the enterprise operating without enterprise modelling.

The investment while initially larger to start the EM modelling practice, decreases in time and becomes stable equalling the difference between the relative costs of running the enterprise without EM and with EM.

Similarly, the relative revenue grow from nil to reach the relative value between the with and without EM cases.

The red line shows the overall benefits by adding the relative costs to relative revenue.

We calculate the Costs and Revenues of the enterprise for the cases in which

- the enterprise has been transformed according to EA principles to reduce the architecture debt, assuming benefits of p% cost reduction and p1% revenue increase vs the usual case costs and revenue
- we continued as usual, without EA clean-up

$$\text{Costs}_{arch} = (1 - p)\ \text{Costs}_{noarch} \qquad\qquad \text{assuming } p = \% \text{ cost decrease}$$

$$\text{Revenue}_{arch} = (1 + p1)\ \text{Revenue}_{noarch} \qquad\qquad p1 = \% \text{ revenue increase}$$

$$\text{RoEA} = (\text{Revenue}_{arch} / \text{Costs}_{arch}) / (\text{Revenue}_{noarch} / \text{Costs}_{noarch})$$

$$\text{RoEA} = (1+p1)/(1-p) = 2, \qquad\qquad \text{assuming } p = p1 = 33\%$$

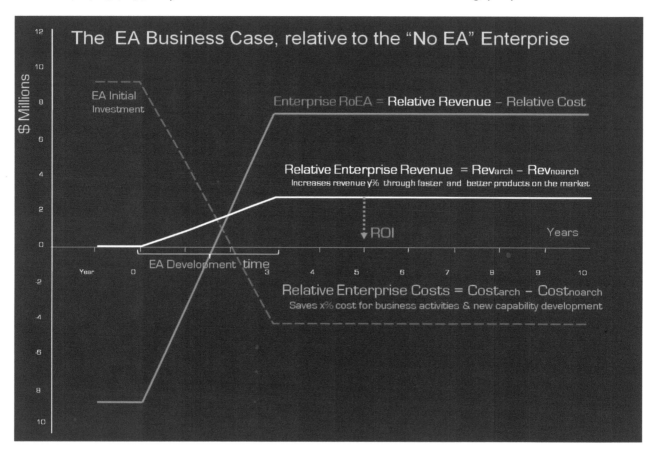

EM Setup -3 Set-up the Enterprise Modelling Development Process

.1. Define EM, mission, outcomes and scope

.2. Specify practice governance and organization

.3. Define EM framework, metamodel & principles

.4. Specify EM development Process and best practices

.5. Select tool , embed framework, organise site

.6. Capture information on existing organization, products, stakeholders, strategy, objectives, business and operating models, roadmapping…

The process is iterative, going in further depth as new entities and views are added.

EM Setup -4 Elaborate first 100 days Enterprise Modelling plan

The plan establishes the key activities and deliverables for the first 100 days. It utilises the same layers as the EM Framework, i.e. Business, Technology and People. At the end of the period, the EM practice (team, organisation, roles, responsibilities) should be built, modelling tool selected.

	People	Process	Technology	Strategy	Deliveries & Measures
Assess 30 days	Meet key ICT and business stakeholders Do presentations to stakeholders to pave the way to EA Do 121s to assess existing team capability	Review existing projects and processes impact on EIA Discover Enterprise overall operation and organization	Assess existing technology and architecture information Review existing infrastructure and apps design Do the Table architecture exercise for discovery: exhibit all existing diagrams on a table	Review strategy and annual plan Review Cloud strategy and e-services (Cloud Sense...) Assess existing applics/platform and obsolescence	Team skills assessed and published Delivery Projects and Processes evaluated Architecture docs reviewed and EA site created Team responsibilities determined Table architecture discovery done Strategies reviewed
Prepare 30 days	Set internal governance: assign team roles, points of contact & project responsibilities Establish individual objectives Recruit to fill in skills Publish EA team role and skills profile Plan and procure EA training Allocate resources to EA work and projects	Create EA site taxonomy Establish architecture domains Create this 100 days Action Plan Establish the 180 days deliveries Select EA tool	Select EA method, principles and metamodel Initiate One Page EA Initiate Information architecture Initiate applications architecture Initiate Infrastructure Architecture	Assess company and ICT priorities Evaluate strategic opportunities, trends	This 100 days Action Plan produced Draft metamodel Site created Training selected Tool selected Framework/method defined Architecture streams initiated Resources allocated to modelling Workstreams initiated
Deliver 30 days	Do EA training Do team building Establish stakeholder map Do EA communications to sell it	Implement EA checks in - Solution/Capability delivery proc - New Product Development - EA inserted in change request process Create EA governance board at ICT and company level Deliver next steps plan	Develop solution architectures Produce One Page Operations Architecture	Produce obsolescence roadmap	Apps obsolescence catalogue Strategy gap Analysis EA communications executed EA tool deployed Training performed Key stakeholder map done Metamodel in tool Next steps plan
100 days Obj.	Develop EA practice Create EA awareness & support	EA controls approved in Business delivery process	Enterprise Architecture baseline created and approved	Enterprise and ICT strategy and plans reviewed	EA Practice created Enterprise One Page Architecture delivered
6 Months Obj.	Train team (on the job) in EA strategy and road mapping	Document and implement EIA development process	Target Single Page Operations Architecture	ICT Roadmap and Strategy approved	ICT Roadmap and One Page target Operations Architect.

Relevant ICT EIA 20XX Objectives
- To align ICT Strategy with Business Strategy
- To produce the ICT Enterprise Architecture and Roadmap

EM Setup_-5 Organise the Enterprise Modelling Practice

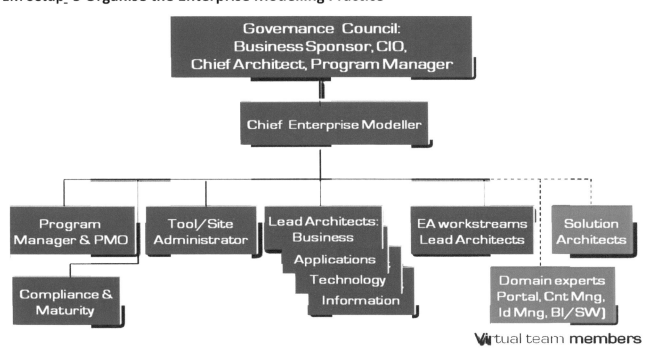

EM Setup -6 Establish key tasks and deliverables

Models the enterprise

- creates or adapt an Enterprise Modelling Framework and metamodel

- establishes an EM Development Process and Best Practices

- establishes the Modelling Standards, Principles and Guidelines

- selects and customises tools

- model the current and target Enterprise states

- specifies the Enterprise transformation roadmap

Manages and integrates modelling activities

- organises the EM team and site and plan activities

- measures EM progress, maturity and value delivered

- organises collaboration and coordinates modelling activities

Communicates and facilitates the enterprise transformation

- communicates with all stakeholders

- coordinates stakeholders' efforts to model their own domains

- assists Enterprise Transformation.

The Enterprise Modelling function organisation

The enterprise modelling may start as a project that establishes the practice: the mission, team, organisation, governance, budget, tools, site, communications structure. The team would develop or select and adapt an enterprise modelling framework, terms of reference, development process, best architecture practices, standards and principles and the first draft of Enterprise Model. The project may then roll over in a Business As Usual (BAU) activity that delivers in further depth blueprints, that ensures the solutions development, integration and conformity to modelling principles and assists the Enterprise Transformation programme in the implementation of the target enterprise state, in conformity with the enterprise roadmap.

The model discovery, documentation, target design, roadmapping, planning and implementation require collaboration of all concerned and expert parties in the organisation. The Enterprise Modellers specify the framework, rules, constraints, diagram types, symbols, principles and standards and then they design the enterprise wide blueprint. They organise and coordinate the work to make sure that stakeholders' deliver artefacts that fit into the whole because the stakeholders in the know and in charge of operating the various functions are responsible for modelling their own domains taking into account the modelling framework rules. They create the enterprise repository consisting of all the components of the enterprise.

The Modellers, employing the EM, may also assist the enterprise in tactical developments such as bottleneck elimination, malfunction fixing, solution design etc

Still, the EM practice is not meant to fix all enterprise problems but to enable their fixing.

The business strategy directions are still set by the Strategy team. The EM team has to gather though and consolidate the top management, departmental strategies and the technology strategies in one single coherent Enterprise level Strategy and then map it to the capabilities of the enterprise, employing the enterprise model.

Still, the strategy planning and implementation effort is lead by the Program Management team and the enterprise architects do the enterprise wide IT architecture, the EA, part of EM.

The Enterprise Modelling deliverables

- The integrated business, organization and technology blueprints of the Current, Transition and Target Enterprise states that can expand to a number of diagrams at increasing level of detail
- A consistent enterprise roadmap and strategy, mapped to the enterprise model and capabilities
- The architecture principles and standards for enterprise transformation
- Assistance and consultancy in solving the Enterprise issues, change and transformation
- Establish architecture Controls in the enterprise transformation and change processes

EM Setup_-7 Set up the Enterprise Modelling site

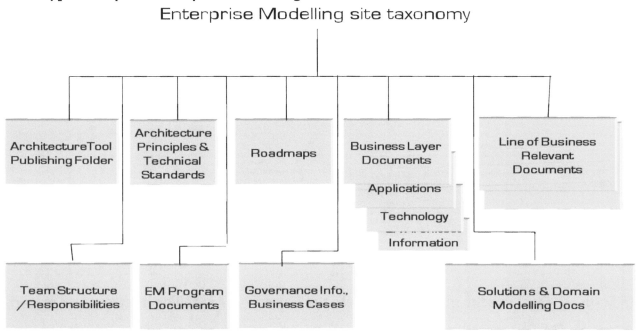

The sample organisation is self explanatory.

EM Setup_-8 Establish EA governance points in enterprise development processes

In each phase of a new product or capability development life cycle establish checkpoints so that the designers stop and consider the application of the recommendations or else emit a waiver. EA shall be gradually employed by all people in the Enterprise.

Specific architectural views though will be documented and designed based on stakeholders and projects priorities. EM controls should be incorporated into business and technology change and development processes.

The Product/Capability development process for instance will have to observe EA enforcement points at each milestone.

Projects will have milestones checked against the architecture deliveries templates. An EA team will still observe all developments for compatibility with the EA and its Framework.

Solution development process with EM controls

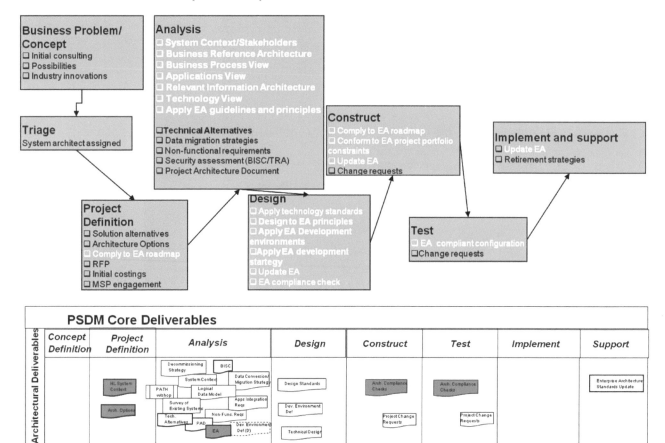

EM Setup -9 Establish the methods to assess the Enterprise Modelling progress and maturity

Measure EM/EA progression in terms of deliveries according to plan

- o Stage 0: Pre-EA
- o Stage 1: EM Program definition. From approved business case till the EM organization is set up, planning and resources are committed and EM architect, Steering Committee and governance are agreed... Capabilities for design and execution are committed now. Should be achieved in set up phase.
- o Stage 2: EM Definition; until the EM framework and tools are established, the As-Is Architecture is discovered, intermediate stages and To-Be EM are sketched, transformation plan approved, KPIs, (Key Performance Indicators) CSFs (Critical Success Factors) and quick wins are determined.
- o Stage 3: Transformation Execution; execution in iterations until 80/20% (functionality/effort) achieved and value delivered confirmed.
- o Stage 4: EM exploitation stage, while incremental design/plan/ implementation stages are still executed.

Measure EM/EA maturity at each iteration in terms of its utility and adoption

- o Level 0: EM ignored
- o Level 1: Empirical EM exploitation
- o Level 2: Documented EM exploitation process
- o Level 3: Managed, used for decision making, change

40

o   Level 4: Optimising EM, improving it

EM Setup-10 Transit the Enterprise Modelling project to Business as Usual work

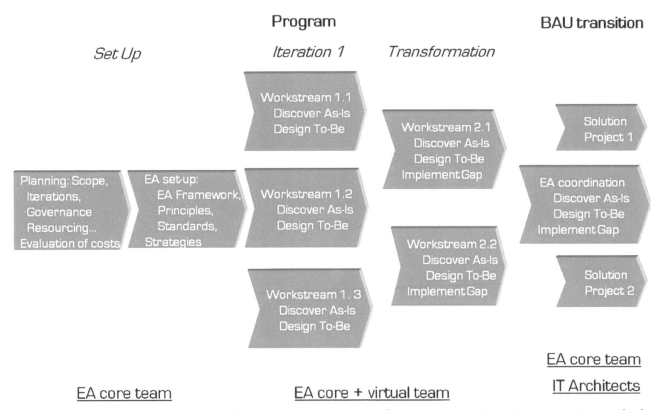

The Enterprise Models, current and target, are constructed in successive iterations, starting with the development of the high level domain or capabilities blueprints and continuing with the in-depth design needed by stakeholders. The initiative typically starts as a project and rolls over into a Business As Usual (BAU) activity after the creation of the practice and the delivery of the initial modelling framework and principles. The BAU activity delivers the EM in iterations, monitors progress and value delivered and assists in the Enterprise Transformation programme that delivers the target enterprise state in alignment to the EM roadmap. The process of building the Enterprise Architecture is iterative, going into depths and adding new entities and views as EM is conquered.

MODELLING CURRENT ENTERPRISE STATE, THE MODELS POSTER

This section establishes Of-the-Shelf reference models to be used as templates and their modelling sequence. Follow Modelling guidelines. Do:

- UML Use Case and scenario diagrams
- block diagrams for Business Reference Maps (functions maps)
- swimlanes/sequence charts and BPMN for Business Processes modelling
- class diagrams or entity relationship for the information architecture and metamodel

Use office tools or choose a free EA tool until you decide what is best for your effort. Establish in advance drawing conventions

- symbols, naming, colour, diagram size, identification box, logos...
- an object appears only once in a diagram and in the repository

1. MS-1 Specify Enterprise Context and Use Cases

Identify key stakeholders and scenarios that are the interactions with them, the customers, shareholders/owners, regulatory, banks, suppliers, partners...

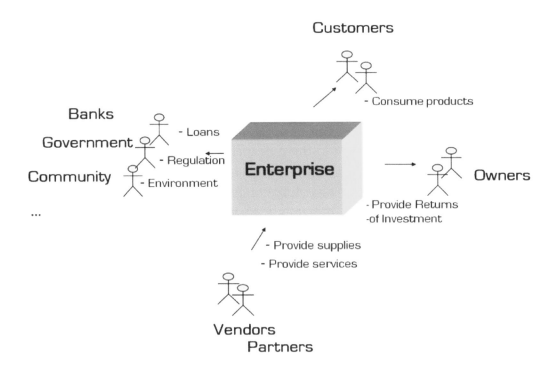

Most enterprises have more Lines of Business each with its value chains; e.g. an airline may have Freight, Catering, Loyalty. Determine the internal Lines of Business (LoB) each delivering a product to a customer segment. For each LoB identify the Value Chain.

2. MS-2 Document GODS Functions and Value Chains for each LoB

Document Lines of Business

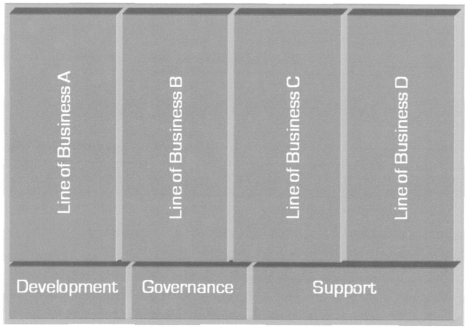

- **Governance** coordinates all other functions

and makes major decisions. Governance boards: Company Board, CEO office, Strategy Board, Risk Management... that make decisions taking into account the company Values, Principles, Policies...... The Governance function is essential because it identifies the enterprise when all other functions are outsourced.

- **Operations** Value Chain (delivers the product)

Portal, Sales and Service, Call Centre, Sourcing and Supply Chain, Access Control, Content and Information Mng...

- **Development** implements new products and capabilities

It also looks into the enterprise evolution. It develops products, capabilities, the enterprise...). Consists of R&D, New Business Development, Organisation evolution, Product Development, IT solutions development, Program Management,

- **Support** services all Lobs and functions in the enterprise

HR, Payroll, Finance, IT support, Legal & Regulatory, Facilities... HR recruits and trains people, manages training, performance appraisal, benefits... The IT function procures and manages technology. Facilities manage real estate and fleet. Finance plans, procures, measures and controls budgets.

Document the Operations Value Chains for each LoB

The Operations capability of GODS consists of the Value Chain capabilities:

.A. **Marketing & Planning (market analysis and production planning)**

- It researches the markets to determine product characteristics, appeal and market size determining specific customer segments and size of opportunity. The Planning part of the function plans to prepare the production and the enterprise for delivery.

.B. **Make & Delivery (make and deliver the product)**

- The capability Sources the parts, Makes the products by assembling the parts and distributes them to outlets. The model adheres to the SCOR - Supply Chain Operation Reference – map: Source, Make and Deliver.

Since most capabilities and functions interact with the customer, do utilize the Model-View-Controller (MVC) paradigm in structuring their architecture to partition it in:

- **V**iew: Channels
- **C**ontrol: Business core logic
- **M**odel: Data organisation

A back tier of Sourcing/B2B that links the function partners and suppliers may be added.

.C. Sell & Service (sell and service the product)

Sells the products, services them and manages customers' issues (After Sales).

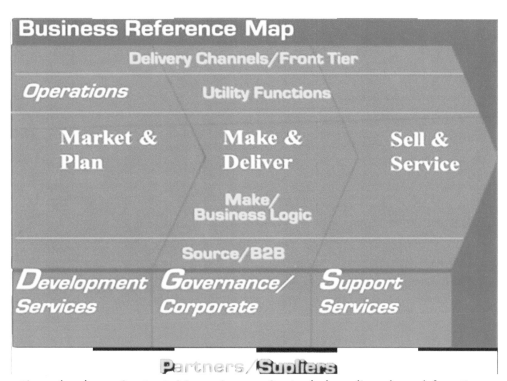

Utility functions (such as Content Mng., Access Control...) realise shared functions such as Access Control, Content Management... The abstract/logic Functions are performed by people and/or technology in lower layers. Some are implemented by IT alone. Since they have no specific outcomes but are just groupings, the entities described are just Functions rather than Capabilities. Each LoB has a Value Chain, a Capability that is, which has a Business Model. Add further stakeholders and scenarios, Lines of Business, Value Chains in iterations.

3. MS-3 Design the single page Business Architecture for each Line of Business

While built on the Business Reference Map, the one page Business Architecture (BA) emphasises not only the static functions but also the Flows (Value Streams), the dynamic components of the enterprise. Flows illustrate the movement of parts and information and their processing in Functions.

Specify the key Operations Flows

The Planning Flow

begins with the market investigation, followed by forecasting to plan for all Operations, Development and Support cycles.

The Demand Creation Flow

stimulates the market, through various channels, to acquire the products

The Production Flow

or Supply Chain delivers the Products, from sourcing to distribution

The Demand Flow

or Sales & Ordering is the process through which the customers obtain the products

The Revenue Flow

or Money Flow charges the customers at sales and ordering, bills and invoices them and accrues the revenue attained for the firm

The After-Sales Flow

or Customer Services for customers' feedback/complaints, product returns & repairs.

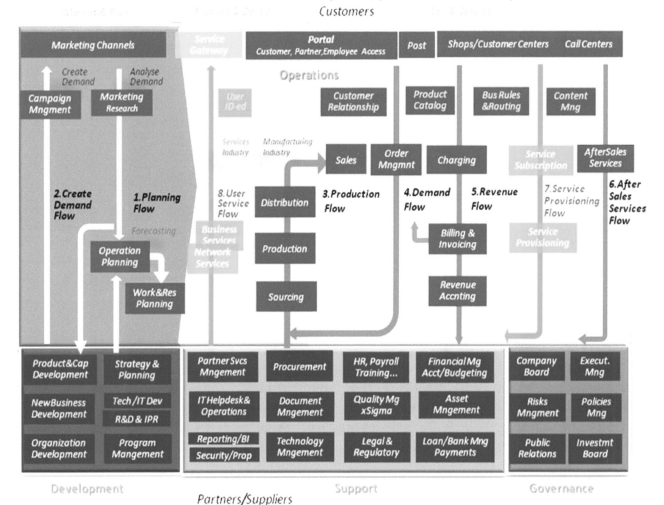

Two (lightly coloured) flows are shown for enterprises that provide online services.

From a Capability viewpoint, the one page BA, illustrates the major generic capabilities any enterprise consists of: Create demand, Plan production, Manufacture the product, Sell, Deliver the service, Provision Service, Process Demand, Account Revenue, Service the products. Each capability consists of a few Functions and Flows. There are variants indeed (see SCOR) where products are sold from stock without the Ordering capability.

The generic BA illustrates the structure/Functions and behaviour/Flows of the enterprise.

4. MS-4 Outline other key enterprise Flows

Any Enterprise operation can be described by a few key Flows such as From...To range of processes. This would be the starting point for the discovery and design of the Process Map. There are external Flows, interacting with stakeholders and internal flows.

Customers' interactions flows

Market Research

Market Campaign

Service Discovery

Service subscription

Service Update

Service Authorisation

Service Usage

Market & Planning flows

From Prospect to Customer

From Market Analysis To

Segmentation to Customer Proposition

From Forecast to plan

From Brand Promotion to Benefits

Make & Deliver flows

From Source to Inventory

From Stock/Order to Delivery

Make to Order

Sales & Service flows

From Product Discovery to Sale

From Sale to Delivery

From Sale to Revenue Recognition

From Order to Invoice to Payment

From Call to Service

Development flows

Idea to Concept to Product...

Strategy Design

Governance flows

From Issue to Decision...

Support flows

From Intrusion to Safety

From Issue to Fixing

From Regulatory to Compliance

Asset Acquisition to Depreciation

Accounting to Reporting

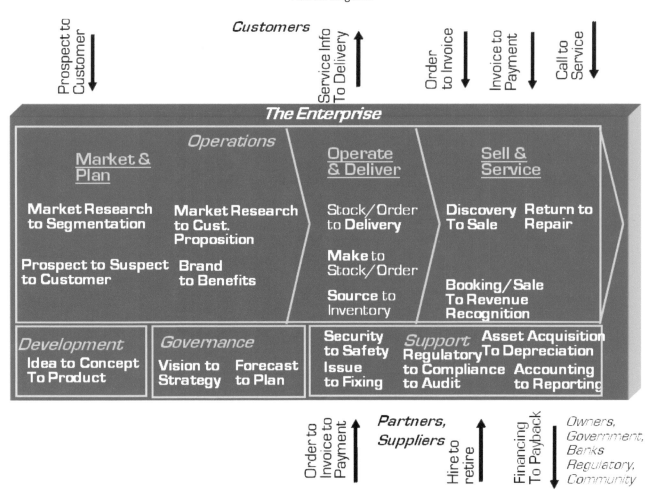

5. MS-5 Specify Information in each Business Function

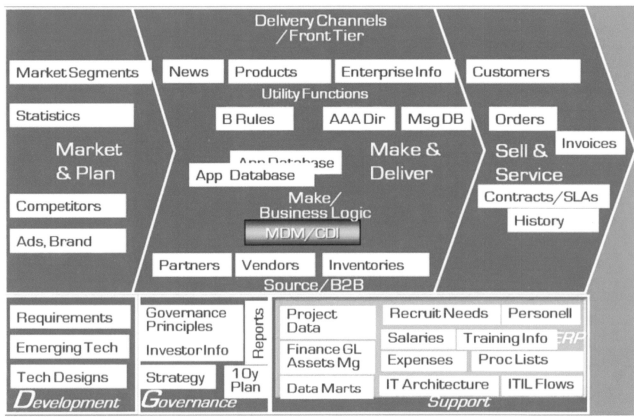

Business information is contained in Functions and processed by Flows. Key information topics in the enterprise have to be mapped to a reference Business Map.

6. MS-6 Design Applications Map on Business Reference Map and do App Catalogue

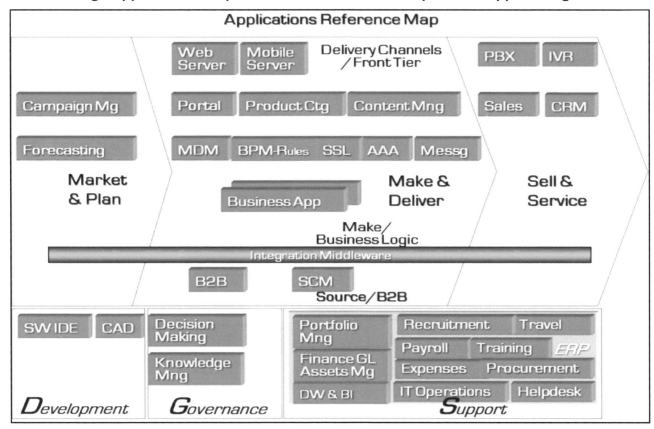

LoB basic Applications catalog

Application Domain (IT template)	Application	Business Function	Technology Platform/ Server	Licenses/ Outsourcing	Life cycle position	Roadmap (link)	Owner Maintenar Developer	Recomed Platform
Distribution	App 1	Sales	Java EE	Mng Serv.	End of Life	www...	Org Role	Oracle...
	App 2							
Presentation								
AAA								
Collaboration Messaging								
Integration Orchestrat.								
Data/Content Management								
Business Logic, B2B								
Support Finance, HR								

The model exhibits the top level view alone. The template provided shows a few typical applications for each Function. Some application suites cover more functions.

Many of these applications are rather standard in that most enterprises employ them. The only parts specific to the enterprise are those that provide the core business logic of the enterprise. The end diagram will show application components in interconnections. The non-IT technology diagrams should be designed at this stage.

Provide an applications catalogue bottom up working with the IT support databases.

7. MS-7 Model technology Infrastructure (Servers, Storage and Networks) around Workplaces

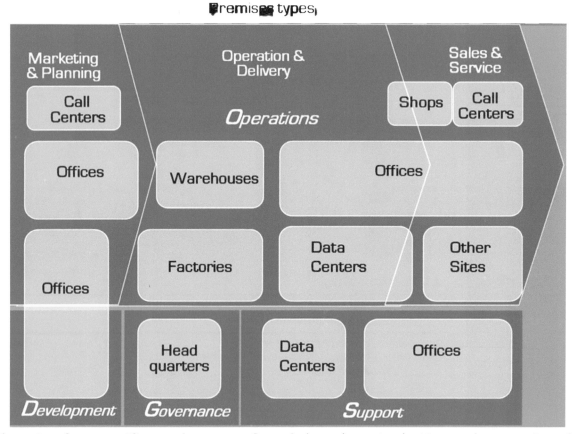

Technology is often specific to the type of workplace (premises). Hence documenting the IT infrastructure on types of premises as in the model makes sense.

Any enterpriseInfrastructure technology can be partitioned on Workplaces:

Head Office, Offices, Call Centre, Data Centres, Factories, Warehouses, Shops, Canteen, Lobby...

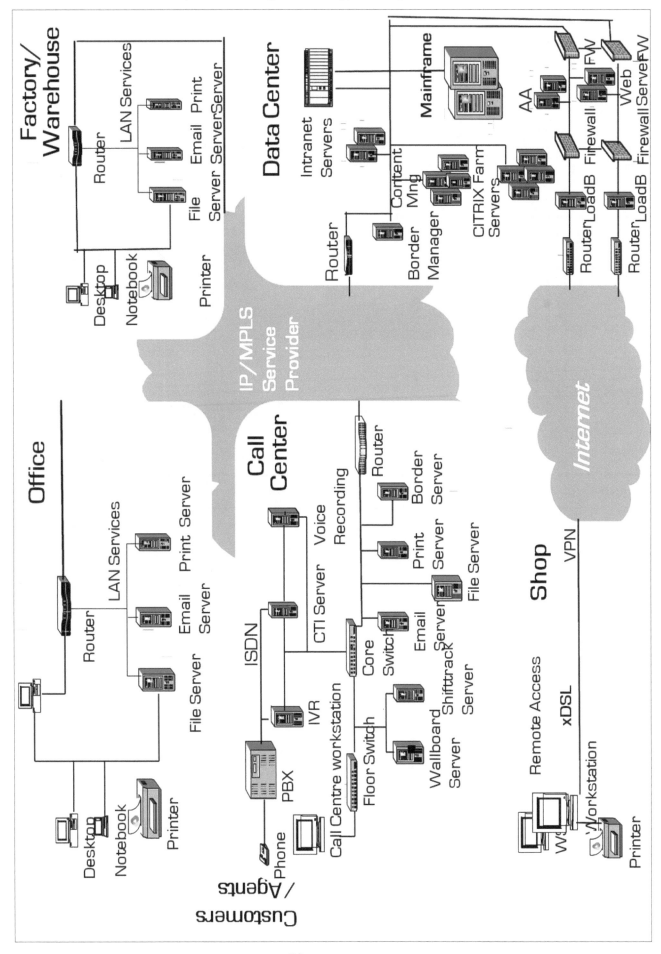

8. MS-8 Map non-IT technology components to Business Functions

to illustrate Voice networks, Data Networks such as ATM or Frame Relay communication technologies etc. They may also describe production bands, electricity grids or water pipes networks.

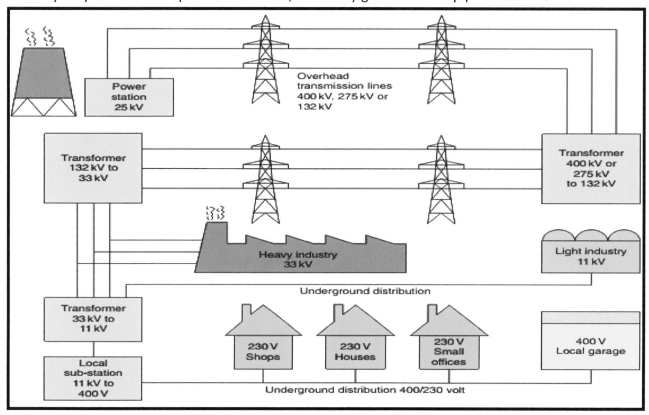

And from http://electrical-engineering-portal.com/general-principles-of-electricity-supply-systems

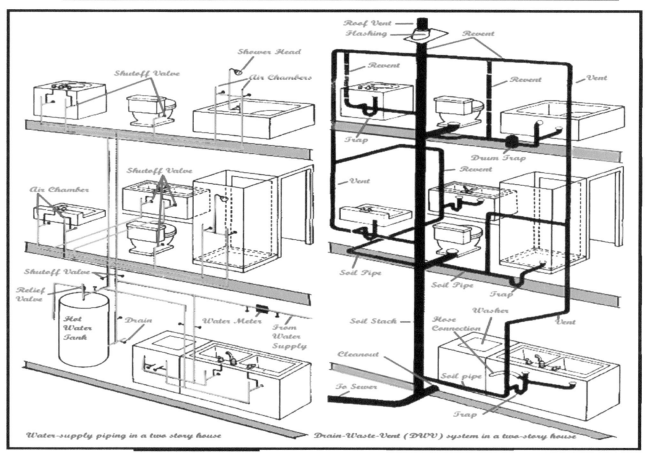

9. MS-9 Re-align organisation chart to Business Functions Map, Workplaces and Locations

The organization chart is often designed around Line of Business, logical Functions, workplace and/or geographical Locations. Map and compare organisation chart to the business functions map with a view to align the two. The end result should be the alignment of the organisation chart to the Functions Map. Also it is good to map Workplace types against Organization since that shows the types of Infrastructure in each location. The Applications map, typically executing business function processes, can also be mapped at last to organisation units so that ownership can be assigned.

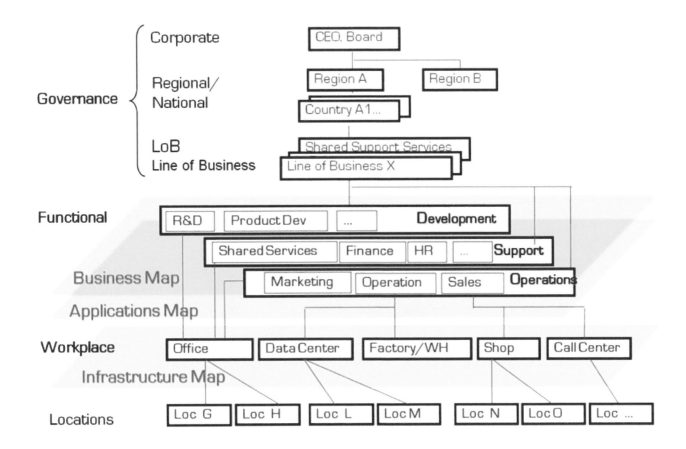

10. MS-10 Design Enterprise wide Views: Security, Location, Performance, Financials...

11. MS-11 Integrate all models into Enterprise Model, prove navigation

The models are built around the functions from the customised reference Business Map and as such these blueprints align and can be navigated end to end. Here is how such a stack of diagrams are navigated following a Flow.

You may visualise a process in a Function. Then you may want to navigate to the technology that implements a process and/or the people that execute it, which navigation would place the observer in either the relevant technology blueprint or the organisation role in a chart. Then come back and track the process again and click on a link to the technology.

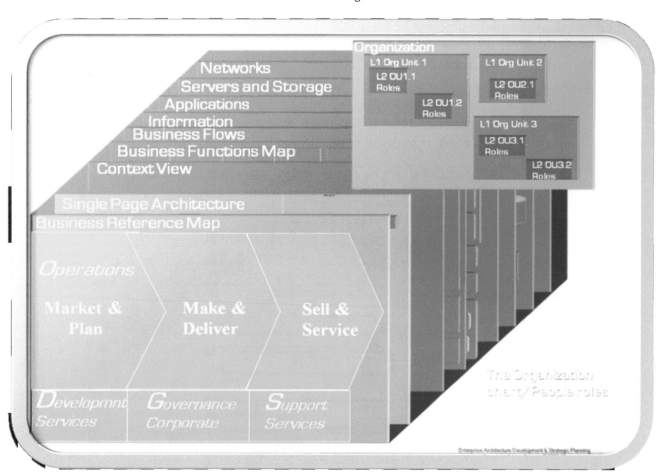

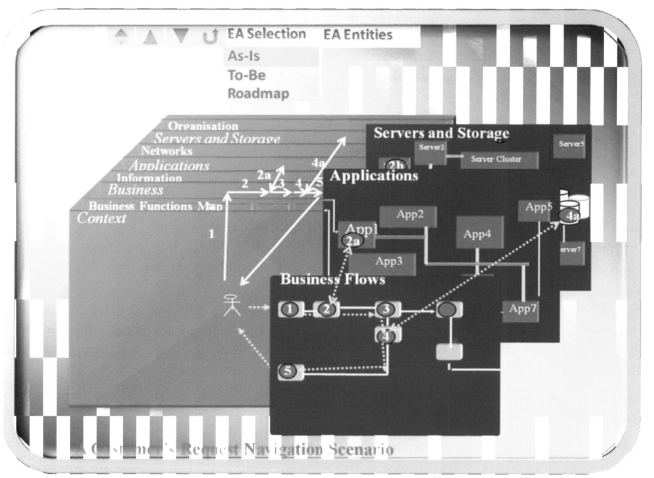

A Customer's Request Navigation Scenario

ENTERPRISE MODELLING FUNCTION BUSINESS AS USUAL ACTIVITIES

W-1 Establish Deliverables and Value Proposition for iteration

W-2 MODEL THE CURRENT ENTERPRISE STATE (see next Chapter)

W-3 Measure EM Progress and Maturity

W-4 Communicate Model, collect feedback from Stakeholders

Iterate from W-1

W-5 Update Enterprise Model/Architecture with Solution Architectures as they are built

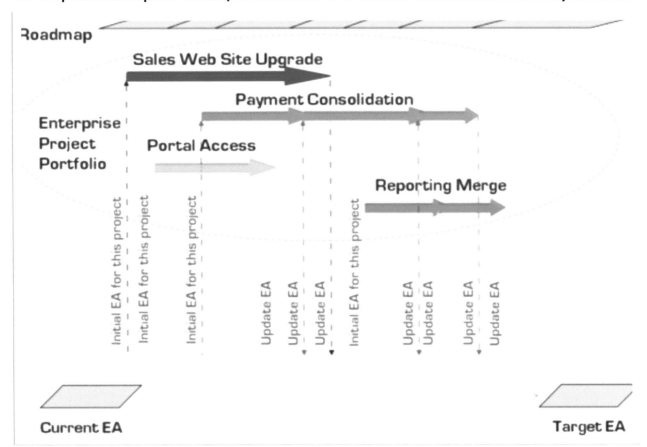

Many projects change your Enterprise structure. The Enterprise Architecture itself (EA), reflecting the

Enterprise structure, evolves, changes with each successful project even if not documented.

Every project has a timeline delivering at various implementation milestones, starting from an As-Is state of a few systems in the Enterprise towards a To-Be state.

Today, a project has to take into account all the concurrent changes, outcome of all other implementation projects, through many to many communication channels. With an Enterprise Architecture in place, every project documents in the EA the planned and actual changes so that all other projects can take stock of changes in the current architecture as soon as planned or take place.

Projects will be mapped on the business and systems architecture to analyse impacts and dependencies. A Project/Solution architecture consists of the same views as the Enterprise Model: Stakeholders' interactions, Business Functions, Flows, Applications, technology, organisation roles...

W-6 Design and Update Enterprise Modelling Framework, Organization, Process. Standards...

W-7 Review Solutions Architecture

W-8 Participate in Enterprise Strategy Design and Enterprise Transformation

ENTERPRISE TRANSFORMATION: TARGET STATE MODELLING, THE PROCESS POSTER

Any enterprise transformation should begin with Enterprise Modelling.

Tr-1 Set out the Drivers for Enterprise Transformation

Business Drivers /// Why,Who, Actions	Customer Satisfaction	Operations Streamlining	Financial Fitness	Strategic Strength	Corporate Social Responsibility Legal
Rationale	Increased Competition Customer Churn	Point Solutions Patching Tame Organic Growth	Revenue Growth Cost Reduction	Cope with amount of information, rate of change, complexity	Increasing Care for the World around
Stake-holder	Customer	Company	Owner	Employee, All	Community/ Government
Business Actions	Improve Response, Usability Develop New Products and Markets	Simplify Legacy Business Process Improvement Align organization	Prioritize investment Reduce costs	Establish Competitive Advantage Manage Change Manage Innovation Turn Digital	Manage Community/ Environment Manage Compliance to Regulatory
Resulting IT Priorities	Single Customer View (MDM) Self Service Engagement through On line sales Social Media	Fix Spaghetti Architecture Straight Thru Processing Cloud Virtualization of Technology One Voice and Data network	IT strategy alignment Single Version of Truth-DW/BI Real Time Business Intelligence	Manage Agility/SOA Risk Management Emerging Technologies Knowledge Management Information Management	Save the environment (recycling...) Community Involvement Disaster Recovery

Tr-2 Establish enterprise Transformation Best Practices

The Enterprise Model (EM) assists the cross-functional transformation team to:

- Establish Transformation Project Portfolio

- Set SMART Deliverables, CSFs, KPIs to ease control at each iteration
- Specify transformation program guidelines
- Create governance and teams
- Apply change management measures
- Prioritise to deliver the urgent fixes for the Enterprise
- Leverage existing applications and infrastructure
- Involve outsourcing and managed services companies
- Work with Suppliers to package applications as services
- Design Plan and Implement agilely, in iterations, with often deliveries and stakeholders' consultation
- Embed EM controls in all development
- Execute iteration
    - Re-engineer existing processes and technology
    - Implementing new processes, technology, governance ..
    - Continuously manage, risks and roadblocks, Communications, Change adoption

Implicitly available, through navigation should be the matrixes of business Functions versus strategy, applications, infrastructure and non-IT technology, data, people roles and organization. Each layer should be described by increasingly more Views, as the EA work progresses through iterations.

Implement EM as a program and later as an organisation function.

Tr-3 Design the Target Enterprise Model

.1. Compile the applications and technology obsolescence roadmap

.2. Map strategy to Enterprise Capabilities and to Functions, Flows, Organisation and Technology
to derive objectives and performance KPIs

.3. Design target Capabilities/Product views, Business Functions and Flows Map...
the Applications, Infrastructure and non-IT technology architectures

.4. Analyse impact of current projects

.5. Design To-Be Business Functions Map

.6. Model the target Single Page Architecture

.7. Documented target business flows for key stakeholders starting with the customer interaction and products

.8. Devise target Information Architecture (IA)

.9. Model target Data Architecture - mapped to IA

.10. Draft SOA like business services

.11. Draw target Infrastructure inventory: servers, storage and networks diagrams

.12. Draw target people organisation

.13. Do Gap analysis

.14. Produce Enterprise Transformation roadmap

.15. Do Planning of next few EM iterations

Design approach

- o Top-Down to establish the business logic, i.e. Functions and Flows
- o Bottom-Up discovery of existing technology and model processes
- o Middle-out design services to wrap capabilities as business services
- o Apply Architecture Principles and Standards to all design

Deliverables

- o To-Be Business Functions Map
- o Target Capability design views
- o To-Be business flows for key stakeholders starting with the customer and products; ERP modelling
- o To-Be Information Architecture
- o To-Be Data Architecture
- o To-Be applications and infrastructure (servers, storage and networks) diagrams, inventory and interconnectivity diagrams and tables
- o To-Be applications diagrams, mapped to processes in Functions, with interconnections (Outcomes/Lines)
- o SOA business services design for target EA

Tr-4 Organise EnterpriseTransformation Portfolio in Programme

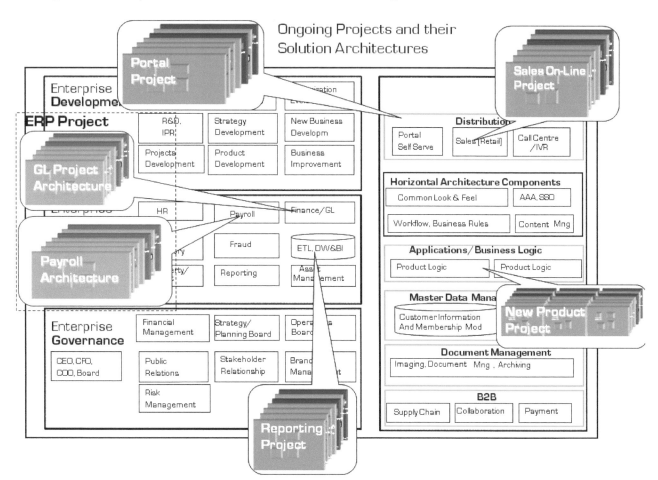

The program includes the projects in scope of the enterprise transformation

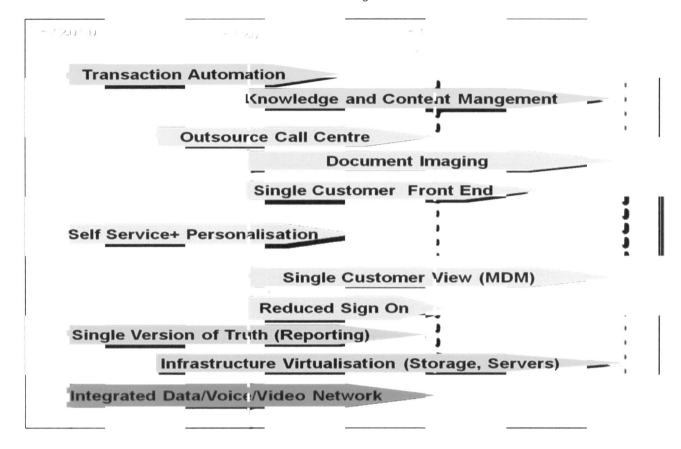

Tr-5 Agree Transformation Plan and Long Term Roadmap

The Enterprise evolves from the current state and mission towards a vision with stated goals and

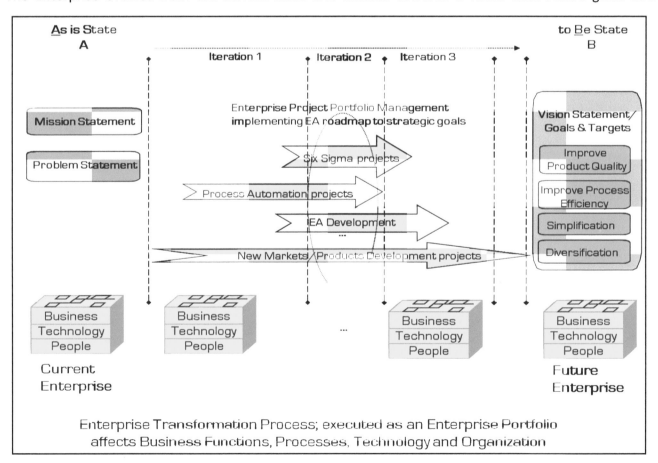

quantifiable objectives. The problem statement clarifies what the problems are and why are you doing it. The Strategic directions (strategies) determine the key programs of transformation by stating in sufficiently general terms what needs to be done to achieve the goals, how the transformation takes place. By implementing the transformation program the Enterprise moves from one state to another towards the visionary state.

The Enterprise Strategy consists of the Business, Technology and People strategies. Business Strategy defines what the business needs to achieve, Technology Strategy, what technology aims to change and replace, and People Strategies are for organization and cultural transformation. Moreover the business strategy should be cascaded to resources, that is to the framework tree layers and elements.

This will be the Enterprise roadmap, the basis of the Enterprise migration plan consisting of an Enterprise project portfolio executing the strategies.

Analyse Enterprise Strategy and plan implementation in every Function. The Business strategy and objectives should be cascaded to Functions, Flows, Technology and People, **top-down.**

Function specific issues are incorporated to Function Strategies for inclusion in the overall Enterprise Strategy, **bottom-up.**

The company will most probably be reorganized to be more effective with regard to the new orientation and goals. To this purpose job descriptions will be redesigned to reflect the impact of new strategies. The culture may be enhanced, new company values may be proposed. Technology will be affected by innovation, simplification and virtualization.

To achieve the future state, the program will transform the EA entities: Functions, Flows and the People and Technology resourcing the Functions.

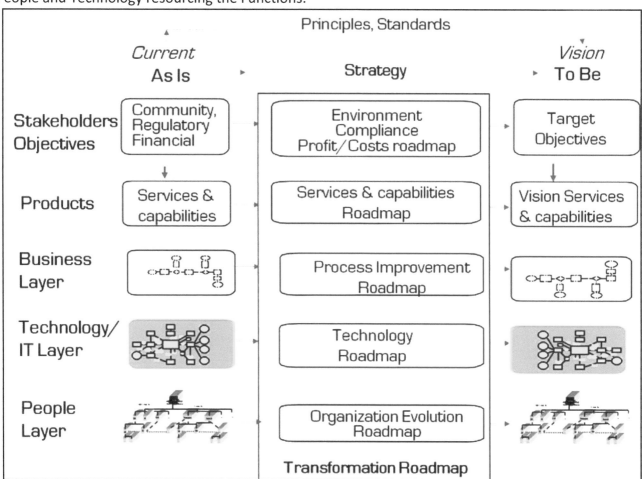

As an intermediary step between business and technology, the Strategy may be cascaded first to the Capabilities of the Enterprise which in the generic case are illustrated in the GODS Business

Architecture: Market and Plan, Produce and Deliver, Sell and Service, Develop, Support and Govern the enterprise. The strategic directions impact on each capability must be evaluated so that the Functions, Flows and Resources.

Tr -6 Cascade strategies to Business Capabilities and Architecture

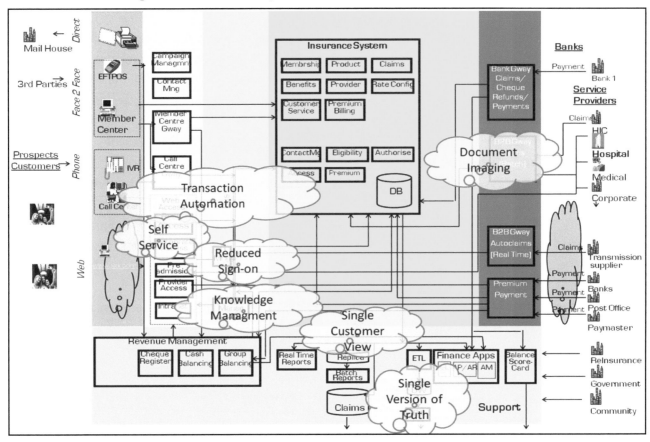

Tr -7 Consider the usual Strategies for IT Applications

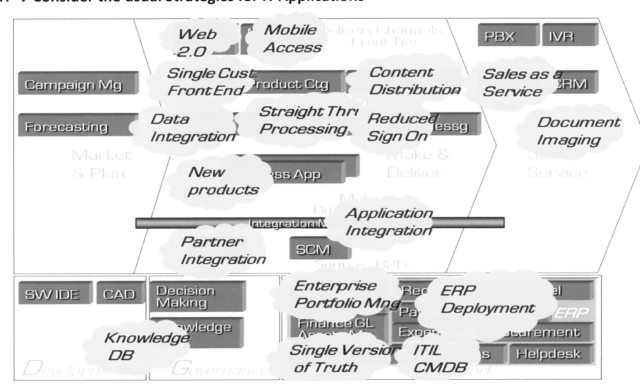

Tr –8 Apply typical IT strategies for Infrastructure Architecture

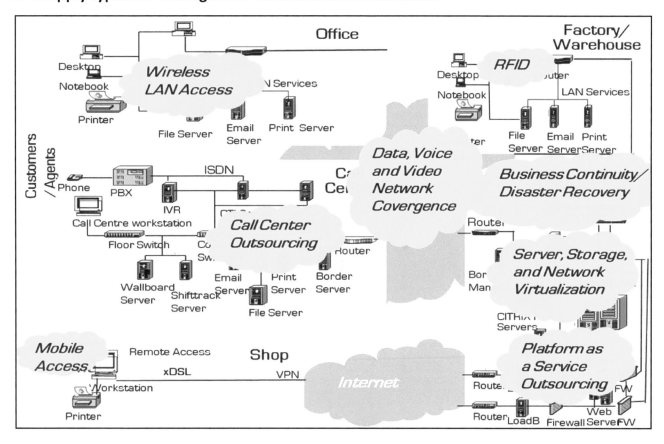

Tr-9 Execute Enterprise Transformation Cycle: Modelling,Transformation, Operation

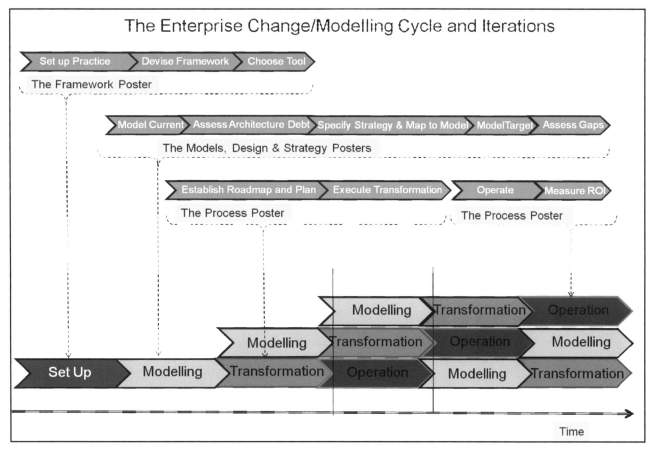

This is the continuous change process that illustrates the fact that modelling takes place in iterations/cycles, in parallel with the enterprise Transformation and Operation.

TR-10 Align Organization to new Business Functions Map

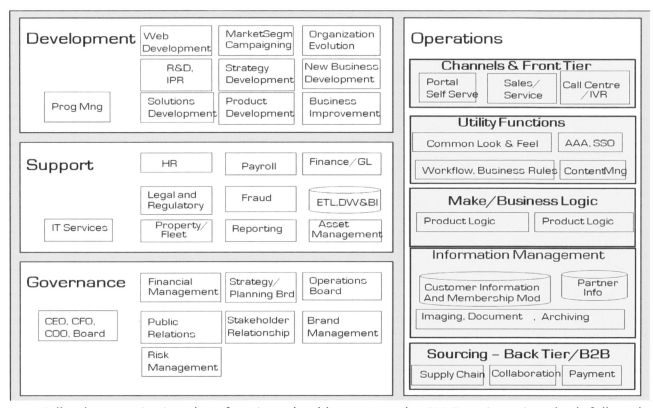

Essentially, the organization chart functions should map over the EM Functions since both follow the

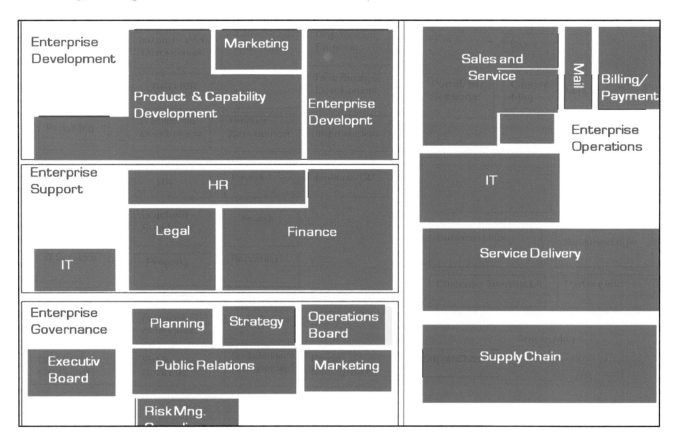

same definition criteria. The hierarchical organization ultimately can be expressed as boxes in boxes, the box higher in the hierarchy encompassing the subordinated function boxes. But the same is true of the hierarchical functions of an enterprise architecture.

Still, geographical location, product lines, end to end processes, customer segments… may sometimes dictate the final organisation of the chart by duplicating functions in geographies or product lines for efficiency. But such considerations may also require the duplication of functions in a geography for instance. Ultimately, it is best for business that the organisational chart and the business architecture stay aligned. The technology and people resources executing a function that belong to the corresponding organisational unit can be better aligned as such due to ownership, community of interests. The enterprise organization should be aligned to architecture to enable ownership of operation of the business Functions by common business and IT teams.

Partition IT in units that reporting to the LoB, except for the truly shared cross boundary processes. The ultimate goal is to unify the business and IT team that deliver the outcome of the function. The people operating the technology should report to the business Function and in dotted line to IT; this weak matrix organization will still enable co-ordination with the rest of IT for technology standardisation and architecture. Align and map the same level of the organisation chart to the matching business functions decomposition level. That would ensure the optimum tuning of the enterprise operation and strategy execution.

MODELLING RECAP

The book proposes an Enterprise Modelling framework, key enterprise reference Models/templates, a modelling sequence to jump start the modelling, an Enterprise transformation process and Strategy design framework and flow. The GODS-FFLV Governance-Operation-Development-Support---Function-Flow-Layer-View framework is the backbone for the Enterprise Modelling.

The key elements of any architecture, no matter the layer, are the nodes and the lines linking them. Both nodes and links are layer specific while they typically implement/execute the functionality of the node and link in the layer above. Nevertheless, at the network level new nodes are introduced that do not map to the business and applications functions.

The Enterprise Modelling in three dimensions, FFLV, and key modelling components

The framework has three dimensions that illustrate the Structure/Functions, Behaviour/Flows and the

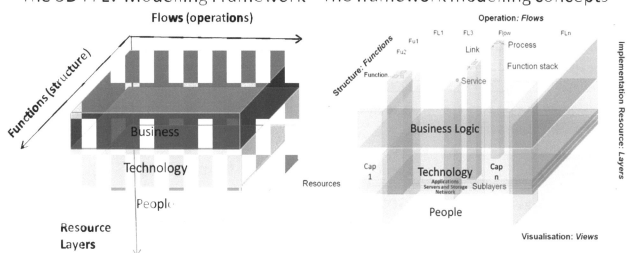

Implementation Resources as three layers: Business/Logic, Technology and People.

Functions (nodes)

are logical grouping of processes/activities. Functions contain rules, information and may have interfaces. Functions, interconnected by Links/Lines, depict the system static Structure; Functions process and store Information and parts.

Flows (Signals)

A flow is a sequence of processes, each executed in the Function it belong to; A Flow delivers an outcome, information or part. The Flows illustrate the system dynamic Behaviour or Operation. They transmit Information and parts between processes in Functions. Their execution is controlled by Rules in Functions.

Layers (Technologies and People)

describing the logical operation and the implementation/resources tiers (technologies and people)

The Enterprise Model can be decomposed as a result on any of the three dimensions, that is on Functions, Flows or Layers.

Functions

logical grouping of processes/activities and the rules, information and interfaces.

Flows

sequence of processes, executed in the Functions the processes belong to.

Functions and Link Stacks

consist in the abstract Function or Link and the People and Technology resources that implement it.The stack can be visualised and navigated on a vertical section through the EM cube.

Capability

is a "can do" ability with an outcome to an enterprise stakeholder or another capability. Its outcome is a service/product the enterprise (internally) delivers. For that, the capability consists of the process, people roles and skills and the technologies that realise it. An enterprise is characterised by a set of capabilities.

To ease mapping and implementation, the enterprise strategy maybe cascaded to the enterprise capabilities which can be planned and implementedseparately.

A Capability can be described by a View consisting of the related set of blueprints illustrating the business logic, - Functions, Flows, Information... - and the resources, people and technology that implement it.

Service

is a capability with a formalised interface that hides the internal operation and technology of the capability.

The enterprise can be also decomposed in capabilities that usually overlap though in that they may be realised by the same systems.

The System/Business logic layer is described in diagrams consisting of Business Functions, their Links and interfaces and Flows (end 2 end processes) executed according to Rules.

The Enterprise generic Structure,GODS

Governance, Operations, Development and Support (GODS) Functions.

Each can be described by a set of Capabilities and Functions.

Since capabilities are embedded in the GODS model they are not explicitly referred to in other instances.

The Technology layer means more than IT, and the People layer is more than organization, that is, includes culture...

Because an architecture consists of nodes in interconnections, the overall Business Architecture is made of the Business Flows executed by Functions.

Begin modelling your one page Business Architecture from the supplied generic logical model (GODS) that illustrates the key Functions and Flows of any enterprise.

A core modelling template

Key reference models

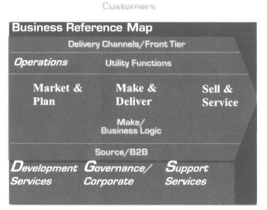

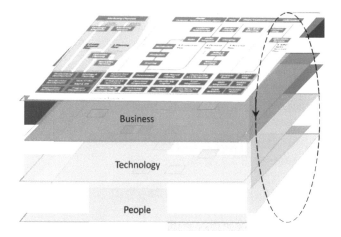

The Enterprise Model Navigation

The visualisation of the model is realised through **V**iews that filter-in only the aspects of concern to a stakeholder, at any particular time. The Views, consisting of Functions, Flows and Information, look like 2/3D sections/CT scans through the enterprise body, the cube.

The GODS-FFLV Framework cube represents the Graphical User Interface (GUI) of the Enterprise Model for stakeholders in search of information, the entry point for navigation. By clicking on stakeholders surrounding the enterprise body or on cube elements such as Functions, Flows, Layers, Views... these elements of the cube can be inspected at various levels of detail.

Equally one may click on the list of Capabilities to select and visualise how a Market Research, Planning, Make, Distribute... or Printing capability, for instance, is implemented in the enterprise.

The enterprise view would be narrowed down to a Capability that can be further browsed on Functions, Flows while Rules and Interfaces can be inspected.

can be done

- vertically between layers, from functional to implementation by people and technology, i.e. from process to application and virtual server plus operating roles or from information to data
- horizontally along processes and interconnections of a Flow, in order to inspect the transmitted entities or the link performance.

An enterprise or capability model can be browsed by selecting

- a function and then inspect a process, Interface and the implementation in the function stack
- a connection/line, the details of which and implementation in the physical layers can be displayed; as for instance an electronic transfer of an Order over an HTTP/TCP/IP connection or a part moving over a production band.

The GODS-FFLV framework is open in that it allows for and integrates any future components, connections or functions, technology and organisation views of interest to stakeholders. Since the cube model representation "contains" the whole enterprise from start, any new elements and views are integrated as long as they comply with the framework principles and constraints.

It's like in an architectural description of a house where you can add views such as plumbing pipes or the electricity network at any time later because they may be there already or they just need to be built and illustrated. As such it allows for growth, scaling and smooth progress in completing the modelling. Take, for instance, the addition of a meeting rooms map, the local network View or a

Financial View exhibiting various Business Functions as cost/profit centres.

The EA framework is in fact a Model Driven Architecture (MDA) with the design starting at the abstract business logic level, the business architecture, going down to the technology and people executing the logic.

The EM metamodel, illustrated in a rather IT specific entity relationship diagram, consists of all component types of an architecture diagram and their relationships. The metamodel shapes and constricts the type of and components of the diagrams. The metamodel components, beside the framework Nodes and Flows, have been identified as: Links (Lines), Interfaces, Information and Rules. Still these components materialise in every layer in a different form. Hence, any Enterprise Model diagram essentially consists of Nodes, Flows, Links, Interfaces, Information and Rules expressed in terms specific to a resource layer.

The Enterprise Model metamodel

is modular as such consisting of the Business, Technology and People metamodels.

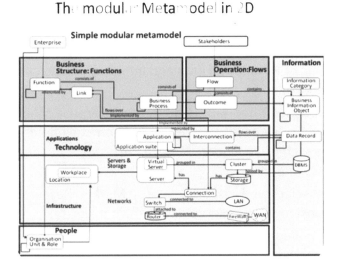

It starts simple with the key elements of the Business layer metamodel. It interconnects Functions and Flows in the Business layer to systems, applications in the technology layer and organisation units/roles in the people layer. The metamodel links the artefacts in the overall one page EM Design. It also constitutes the DB schema of the EM (tool) repository. The metamodel is further elaborated as the EM progresses with additions of partial metamodels such as, for instance, a Business Motivation Model, as sometimes called, which eventually shows the way strategy and vision are mapped to the enterprise model components.

An Enterprise Architecture tool will significantly add to the ease of the EA development and management process, by realising the metamodel in the component repository schema and offering the Enterprise Model, visualisation, navigability, reporting, standard diagramming, and to the transformation process, the tracing of strategy to capabilities and projects.

The Enterprise Model in 2D and the 3D view linked by the Metamodel

Consisting of all key models assembled in a synoptic 2D single page view of the enterprise blueprint. The components of models are interlinked in metamodel relationships.

The metamodel integrated EM

The 3D integrated EM Design

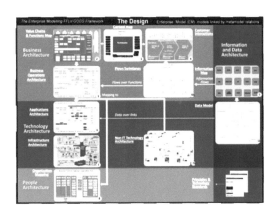

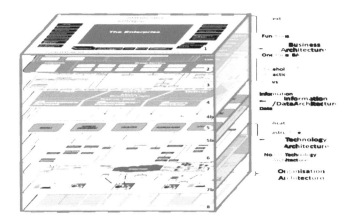

The current Enterprise Modelling Development Process

1. *Model enterprise context: Products and Stakeholders' Use Cases*

2. *Document the enterprise Value Chains*

3. *For each Value Chain employ the reference model provided to*

    3.1. Devise the Functions Map

    3.2. Model key Business Flows

    3.3. Model the one page business architecture using generic model

    3.4. Model the Information Map

    3.5. Model Technology (IT Apps, Infrastructure, non-IT) Architectures

    3.6. Do the Organisation Map

    3.7. Assess Capabilities and model them as Views

    3.8. Do other architecture Views: security, geography...

    3.9. Measure EM progress and maturity

    3.10. Stakeholders employ EM and return feedback

    3.11. Iterate from beginning, improve and add components and detail

The Enterprise Transformation process

.1. Model the target Enterprise

    o Collect Requirements for Target Enterprise and evaluate Strategy

    o Map Requirements and Strategy to Enterprise Model dimensions - Functions, Flows, Layers

    o Design the target Enterprise Modelin terms of Business, Technology and People

.2. Evaluate gaps to current Business, Information, Technology, Organisation... models

.3. Evaluate Business Case for transformation and get approved

.4. EstablishBusiness/Technology roadmap

.5. Establish plan and deliverables

.6. Set-up transformation organization and governance (role JDs, recruit, train...)

.7. Execute

.8. Measure returned value, Iterate

Specify Enterprise Strategy

The Strategy Rings Framework and Process

The strategy development process

- Analyse environment for Opportunities, Threats, Trends
- Analyse current strategy and company for strengths and weakness
- Specify strategies to alleviate threats and take advantage of Opportunities
- Check Strategies for Suitability...
- Balance strategies

The Strategy Rings Framework

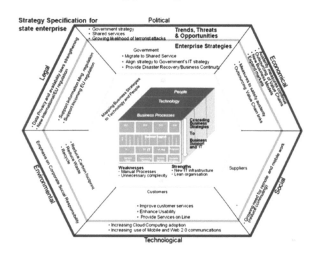

The Strategy Specification Process

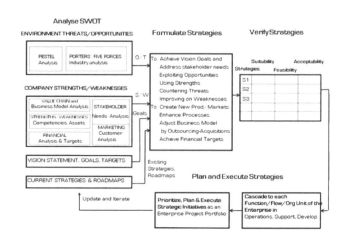

Why use the GODS-FFLV framework

The framework enables you to

1. Define the key elements (nodes, links, Functions....) of any enterprise description/artefact while employing the same concepts as the business: Value Chains, Value Streams, Business Models, Operation Models...

2. Relate and align in the EA framework and provided metamodel the often confusing terms such Process, Functions, Capability, Service, Workflow (Flow: Value Stream)...

3. Establish the key type of modelling artefacts: node maps (block diagrams), class/entity relationship diagrams, swimlane workflows... and the relationships between them (The Design poster)

4. Employ the readymade models (templates) and modelling sequence provided to jump start your design (The Models poster)

5. Describe completely the enterprise structure (Functions), dynamic behaviour (Flows) and implementation (Layers) aspects; any entity of an enterprise model would be as such a Function or Link that belongs to a Flow in the Business or Resource Layer

6. Decompose the Enterprise in an hierarchical tree, navigable by business Function, Flow or Resource Layer or even capability

7. Navigate the Enterprise Model from the cube graphical interface (GUI) by employing menus or clicks on the cube representation elements
   - vertically, up and down across layers to various degrees of implementation detail
   - horizontally, tracking Flows from function to function (system to system) along connections

8. focus on modelling your enterprise rather than (re-invent) the framework as many do

9. cover the whole enterprise rather than only IT, counting in people organization and interactions

10. add in non-IT technology, as many enterprises rely on key technologies other than IT

11. establish a concise common single view of the enterprise for all stakeholders through the One Page Business Architecture

12. create at any later time of any number of further Views of interest to stakeholders such as data, security, location, performance, financials...

13. execute Strategy by cascading objectives to the EM decomposition tree consisting of Capabilities, Functions (GODS), Flows and Technology systems rather than to the People organisation alone

14. Re-use the framework with predictable and similar results.

THE ENTERPRISE EVOLUTION TO DIGITAL AND THE ROLE OF ENTERPRISE MODELLING

The enterprise will evolve to Digital. Automation, digital channels, digitalised products and manufacturing bands (IoT), capabilities outsourced to the Cloud...

The pace of technology change will progressively accelerate and so will be the change of the enterprise. To enable it, the enterprise will have to be constructed out of easily interchanged modules which could be modified independently. Hence the Service Oriented Enterprise. The Virtual Enterprise (VE), "a virtual organization is a firm that outsources the majority of its functions" would emerge.

The processing, storage and networking will be fully virtualised for ease of configuration

The Enterprise various functions would be virtualised, that is hidden behind abstraction layers.

There would be a single type of access, web based, to every application or function.

At the EA business layer, workflows would be implemented by process and rules engines as orchestration of SOA and Web Services listed and described in a catalogue (UDDI, WSDL).

This abstracts away the complexity of IT and its applications under a layer which business people can understand and now model themselves. They would be able to design and change processes using BPEL (Business Process Execution Language), as a composition of SOA and SaaS business services, using graphical interfaces.

For the EA information layer, MDM (Master Data Management) adds a similar virtualization layer since most application will utilize now information provided by this layer rather than supplied by all other applications.

More in the following sections.

The Service Oriented Enterprise

Service Oriented Architecture (SOA) is a design paradigm that helps control system change. Our main problem today is the fast pace of change. SOA promotes modularity and rigorous interfaces while it hides the implementation technology enabling as such breaking out complexity in independently designed blocks. It enables the flexibility and agility required to respond to the greater than ever pace of change. It ultimately enables the Cloud.

SOA was declared dead but it isn't. As an architecture paradigm, it never died. It was reborn in software design, where it was buried in the first place, under the name of micro-services. It is still valid for the enterprise. The Cloud enforces it bit by bit as functionality is gradually outsourced to the Cloud in SOA like services.

What is SOA

But what is SOA? Is it a technology an architecture, a program, or a product? Is it a business or an IT development? What is the rapport to BPM? And what is the relationship to Enterprise Architecture (EA)?

After all, both SOA and EA are about the Enterprise and its architecture, with the EA supposed to remedy similar malfunctions of the Enterprise. It is just that SOA appears to attract an even more IT oriented audience than EA. The question is should we implement SOA and EA, or SOA, or EA, if any?

For most business people, SOA looks like yet another over hyped information technology. SOA, which may have its roots in a long history of distributed components architecture, is usually associated to Web Services technologies and is typically promoted by IT.

Like the OO, SOA is about providing encapsulated data and behaviour, accessible solely through published interfaces. But, as opposed to OO, which addresses the SW development community, SOA aims at services business can understand and orchestrate to implement end-to-end Enterprise processes.

In a W3C definition, SOA is "a set of components which can be invoked and whose interface definitions can be published and discovered."

From an IT point of view, a SOA service is a component providing a service which exposes an interface hiding the internal implementation technology, published in a registry, and dynamically discovered. Web Services have been implementing for a while now the SOA paradigm over Web protocols. As a result, SOA is often associated to Web Services and its technologies (SOAP, XML, UDDI, WSDL...).

But SOA is more than IT although its origins are in IT.

From a business angle, SOA is a style of business architecture design and, ultimately, a way of structuring your business. It enables a Business Oriented Architecture (BOA, a new acronym) by allowing the business define Enterprise workflows around reusable business services. The granularity of the service is targeted at the business cognizant, rather than at the software application developer.

The concept of service is not new; one can find it in the Yellow Pages. An SOA service may not necessarily be implemented by software or provided by IT technology. From a business point of view, one may think of an SOA service as an internal postal service with a pigeon hole interface provided by a team of people, no matter what technology. In fact, services can be performed by human beings and/or other non-IT technologies. A service, as in every day life, is an activity executed by people and/or technology returning value to its consumer for a price.

A business service would require definition and enforcement of SLAs to control the quality of the service delivered and the service consumption within defined usage limits. Security is another important aspect of SOA as it regulates access and enforces privacy and integrity of the information exchange in a distributed environment.

SOA benefits

More often than not, agility and technology reuse are the major benefits associated to SOA. The reality is that SOA, frequently approached outside an Enterprise Architecture context, is developed incrementally, without the benefit of the big picture the Enterprise Architecture delivers. As a consequence, the promised agility is not achieved or achieved late, towards the end of the SOAization of your Enterprise when technology reuse may require costly redesign.

It is worth mentioning though that Business process reuse is the advantage rather than IT, since SOA identifies similar business activities and groups them in a service. SOA reduces process replication and, only afterwards, for the same type of process, the application duplication.

Nonetheless, there are a few other major SOA benefits, which should be more easily achieved, understood, and accepted. Invoking these advantages would make SOA a joyous sell rather than the reported stressing experience.

Business service accountability that improves business governance

Applications and suites, usually a bundle of many functions, provide many services; in practice, a large group of business and IT people will share the responsibilities for the data and behaviour of applications. But who can hold accountable such a group of individuals with many other responsibilities? In such an environment, neither accountability nor authority can be assumed for specific functions in an application. On the other hand, for an SOA business service, there is a specific function or role assigned the responsibility: it does not matter if it is an IT or business issue, there is one single point of contact for the service and an SLA to deliver against.

IT technology virtualization offers contractual interaction

that hide the implementation technology and offers a clear, contractual-like interaction between business and IT. IT becomes a service provider, offering business services at a QoS secured by an SLA, well comprehended, quantified, and eventually remunerated by the business through a payback mechanism. This is a major achievement since your applications and technology are hidden behind IT services with contract interfaces supplied to the business. From a business perspective, this is what really counts. No longer the division between business and IT, but well cut interfaces, SLAs, and contracts. No more blame culture. The separation of concerns pacifies the parties.

Untangling the applications providing a clean architecture, reducing the side effects of change

There is no more random access, through the back door, to parts of applications or databases, which makes any change a burden and any modification of an application a major risk because of unforeseeable effects.

Extended lifetime for your legacy applications, reducing the immediate pressure to replace them

This is achieved through the encapsulation of legacy in a host of services. Although there are other increasing costs related to legacy technology, there is no more pressure to replace it; you can do it at your own convenience when a viable alternative exists. This is an extension of the technology virtualization.

SOA and BPM

The relationship between SOA and BPM has been the subject of debate. No wonder, since there are different professional groups, magazines or activities to address them.

BPM was in vogue in the 90s as BPR, Business Process Reengineering. As a concept it is the practice of discovering your processes, and improving and automating them to reduce human error, delays, and reduce costs. There are notations and languages to describe business processes. There are models that help in evaluating the maturity of processes and frameworks, such as CMM and Six Sigma, for process improvement.

Business processes are also a part of the Business layer of the Enterprise Architecture (EA). The Enterprise processes would be described by current and target process architecture parts of As-Is and To-Be EA. Processes are still abstract in that they still have to be performed by humans and/or machines.

SOA is a style of business process design for the target architecture with processes implemented as a sequence of loosely coupled SOA services. SOA is an evolution of BPM aiming to hide and encapsulate complexity in business services.

In SOA, the business workflows will consist of orchestrated SOA services that encapsulate both the process and the technology implementing it.

From a technology viewpoint, BPM is offered at the EA business layer, as Business Process and rules design, execution and monitoring engines. Now these are offered as part of an overall SOA proposition, since they provide an orchestration service.

On the other hand, SOA is an integration technology based on products as Enterprise Service Buses (ESB), Service Registries, and management tools.

But SOA services definition is still in the realm of business; services should be specified by business people since they are not an IT concern or in the IT domain of expertise. This being said, ERPs, embedding and integrating various Enterprise processes, are the products of IT companies.

SOA versus EA

SOA alone is misleading if not taken in the context or scope of the development. After all, it can be applied to any architecture (an application architecture, for instance) and not necessarily to an Enterprise Architecture (EA).

A note of caution: the Enterprise Wide IT Architecture (EWITA) is often called Enterprise Architecture. SOA harbours under its umbrella developments that are in the scope of EA. SOA does cover architecture, but it does not specifically address business process automation, IT alignment to strategy, even if it helps; it does not document the As-Is state like EA does; and it does not provide guidance for the development program as EA frameworks do.

SOA requires a large Enterprise process re-engineering and re-design effort, with significant consequences, at process, applications, infrastructure, and people Enterprise Architecture layers. Services will be reused, access will be enforced by SLA contracts, and a new SOA services governance will be in use affecting the existing organization and applications suites.

SOA development may hide the recognition and complexity of an EA program, even though it is not an EA "inhibitor" per se. SOA, given its scope and ambition, should be a joint business and IT effort, a key part of a full EA development, and not considered in isolation as a light IT Enterprise Integration effort.

SOA + EA = SOEA

A "Service Oriented Enterprise Architecture," SOEA, defined as an EA with an SO style of target architecture, would better describe the positioning of SOA with regard to EA. EA may be implemented without SOA while a stand-alone SOA development, mainly driven by a Service Orientation Architectural requirement, will tend to ignore business objectives and strategy.

The EA sets in place a process to achieve technology and organization alignment to business processes, strategy, and objectives.

SOA, as a style of business architecture, is adding value to the EA by enabling modularity at the business service level, and, as such, agility, reuse, Quality of Service, facilitating payback mechanisms and service contracts. This means a more decoupled business where services are provided and consumed based on contracts. And this offers enhanced manageability. More, there are benefits from enabling services provided over the Web using Web Services technologies and from making possible service outsourcing on an on-demand basis, such as Software as a Service (SaaS).

SOEA, the development of an EA with an SOA flavour, must have support from top management and involve business since it requires process re-engineering, technology alignment, and firm re-organization, in other words, SOEA transforms the whole Enterprise, more than EA or SOA taken separately.

As both SOA and EA are usually initiated by IT, the lack of business stakeholders' engagement and firm's management support or funding may foil the success of SOEA.

The SOA should be initially implemented as an additional EA service layer – on top of the EA applications layer – which would exist during the Enterprise Transformation stages. Some time into the future, the Applications will be, hopefully, implemented as Business Services, and the SOA services layer will cease to exist. This requires the applications suppliers to adopt SOA, which would be an advantage for everybody except, may be, for them.

Once implemented, SOEA (EA + SOA), becomes a powerful competitive asset since it is the blueprint of a service-based Enterprise, with best of breed components easily outsourced, no matter what technology or geography.

Key messages for the road

- SOA EA is primarily a business development, a way to structure your Enterprise, a style of target business architecture, and only then an integration and orchestration technology.

- SOA EA must have support from top management and involve business since it requires process re-engineering, technology alignment, and firm re-organization.

- Since both SOA and EA are usually initiated by IT, the lack of business stakeholders' engagement and a firm's management support or funding may foil the success of SOEA.

- Pick only the technology you need; after all, SOA is about integration: vendors have piled all their products in the SOA basket – BPM and rules engines, user interaction (Portals), application servers, B2B gateways, messaging middleware, repositories/registries, data management, business intelligence products, development environment and management equipment. They are not selling you a monolithic ERP; SOA is about best of breed services.

- SOA does not succeed outside an Enterprise Architecture development since, in itself, it does not cover the development process, the current situation discovery (process, apps, infra...), information architecture, the alignment to strategy...

- SOA will not succeed without an Information Architecture and service in place because, after all, SOA services will have to use the same vocabulary and documents definition.

- It is still at the top of Gartner's hype cycle so be aware that it still has to reach its plateau of productivity and its market maturity

- SOA benefits
  - provides good business governance with clear accountabilities for business service delivery
  - SOA transforms IT in a business service provider
  - It virtualizes IT applications technology behind service interfaces and subsequently reduces the division between business and IT
  - untangles the applications, removing the random, back door connections
  - extends the life time of your recent legacy through encapsulation
  - when fully deployed, at the Enterprise level, provides reuse and agility
  - enables outsourcing, such as SaaS (Software as a Service)

The Virtualisation of the Enterprise

Porter conceptualized, in the 80s, the Value Chain (VC) of an Enterprise. A VC categorizes the business functions of a company in primary (operations) and secondary (support) functions. Porter also introduced Value Networks or Systems consisting of a string of Value Chains contributing to the delivery of the end product or value where each VC is implemented by a separate Enterprise.

A business model specifies, amongst other, the specific way a firm approaches and segments the market, delivers value to its customers, manages relationships with customers and partners, and customizes its value chain and core capabilities to return revenue.

In what we are concerned with, the business model characterises "the architecture of the firm and its network of partners".

A Business Architecture should be structured on the Value Chain and Business Model of the Enterprise since this is how the business perceives architecture.

To succeed in Today's business world, competition is not enough. Strategic alliances and collaboration are required and partnerships are key. With the pace of competition today, outsourcing becomes an important strategy. And through outsourcing, the supplier company will become part of your Value Chain.

From a technology viewpoint, IT virtualization makes inroads in the Enterprise by decoupling the concerns of business and IT and between applications and technology while enabling outsourcing. Technology virtualization allows the creation of abstract services, hiding their physical implementation and enables their exploitation over generic interfaces.

The Virtual Enterprise (VE)

Many business functions of your organization can be outsourced. What traditionally were considered core functions are no more a sacred territory for outsourcing. The difference in cost and efficiency between an "on demand" or pay per usage outsourced service and an on-premises and self manned typical function could be significant and hard to ignore.

This raises speculation on an Enterprise that outsources most or all its business functions but retains governance for planning, coordinating operations, budgeting and making all key decisions. In a Wikipedia definition "a virtual organization is a firm that outsources the majority of its functions". The Virtual Enterprise (VE) can be successful, assuming it employs best of breed outsourced services in a "virtual" Value Chain implementation consisting of company and partner links.

A VE operates over a virtual Value Chain i.e. a chain whose links are owned by company and partners, blurring the borders between the Value Chain of the firm and the Value Network it is part of.

The Governance is the business function that defines and identifies the Virtual Enterprise since most or all other functions of the Enterprise (primary and secondary in Porter's definition) could be outsourced.

The VE is defined by a new operating model promoting collaboration and B2B to take advantage of best of breed applications on the market. This VE business model is increasingly enabled by the adoption of business process outsourcing (BPO), application outsourcing - Software as a Service (SaaS) - and in general by the fast adoption of infrastructure virtualization technologies, Web Services, SOA and collaborative technologies of the Web2.0.

The "Virtual" Enterprise could be the darling of the entrepreneurial world, specializing in management and governance skills while outsourcing most of the Functions of the Enterprise today.

Today, for historical reasons, the interface between business and IT is quite convoluted and low level, leading to business having to understand and take decisions about IT and IT having to understand the business workings. That's why, when simple business meetings to discuss IT capabilities become debates on the merits of WS SOAP relative to REST, the communication between business and IT breaks down.

Technology choice should be in the IT domain rather than on the business agenda and business should be able to change processes, rules and content directly without IT intervention.

In this fast moving world, the business in an Enterprise, its logic, should not depend on IT technology, that is, its type or implementation. Business activities would be performed careless to technology and fearless to tomorrow's new IT hype. Why bother it is mainframe, COBOL, JavaEE or .NET, Smalltalk, 4GL or AS400 RPG! At the same cost/performance, this should be an IT choice which surely would change in the future.

Business should be willing to adopt technology virtualization to be able to interact with IT technology at a service level where the negotiation between business and IT is performed in a communication language structured in terms of capabilities, relative feature merits and their cost. IT functional and non-functional capabilities will be delivered under SLAs at an agreed price.

IT virtualization is adding an interface layer hiding the IT implementation complexity and technology.

IT virtualization is a significant step forward in patching the divide between business and IT, often materialized in the blame culture, we all know, since business people can then make abstraction of the IT infrastructure, issues, terminology... No amount of good will solve this divide until a good insulation (interface) layer is inserted between the two. Business and IT will talk the language of business: services, QoS, SLAs, capacity, security, a vocabulary they all understand. The business people does not have to talk or understand IT any longer, and vice versa, and could, for the first time, be in charge of business processes.

IT, in turn, becomes a true business service provider negotiating SLAs and licenses, very much like an ASP (Application Server Provider) provider. An IT application suite would be offered as a set of business services now. New services such as, Software, Platform or Integration as a Service recently appeared.

The virtualization of the Enterprise Architecture (EA) layers

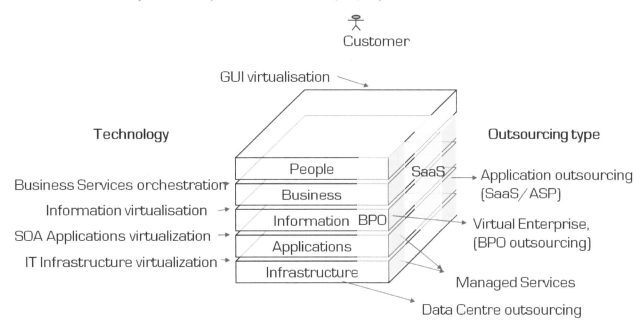

Virtualisation, Outsourcing and the Enterprise Architecture layers

An Enterprise may be described at a few typical Enterprise Architecture (EA) layers: business, information, applications and infrastructure. To these, you might add people/ organization and non-IT technology which are sometimes neglected.

Layers though, can be virtualized. This is the way it is done in the network OSI (Open Standard Interconnect) standard where each of the layers provides services over an interface to the layer above.

In the Enterprise space, the virtualization appears to seep upwards across EA layers, from infrastructure to applications and business processes.

The virtualization of the IT infrastructure

a hot topic now, in the Enterprise, is, quintessentially, about providing an abstraction to the IT technology: servers, storage and networks. It is about an interface layer hiding the infrastructure implementation and its platform types. The benefits appear to be compelling: server utilization grows significantly and inverse proportionally to the number of servers, the cost of the occupied real estate and cooling.

What infrastructure virtualization promises? Independence from the HW infrastructure. Multiple applications and OSs run on one or multiple physical servers. Virtualization is supported by blade systems as well where processing power is modularly scaled.

Processing power can be consumed "on demand" (IBM parlance); MIPS can be purchased in an "utility" like model (HP talk). Storage will be retailed as a commodity from a pool and I/O is ultimately virtualized.

An analogy can be made to the networks world where the leased physical lines evolved into virtual circuits, VPNs etc. where, newly, QoS matters in defining a virtual channel.

Virtualization evolves to "Real Time Infrastructure" that enables configuration, scaling of applications and dynamic allocation of computing resources as dictated by business calendar or load.

Virtualization provides light and less costly business continuity and easier management. Ultimately the infrastructure can be outsourced to a 3rd party and paid per usage. There is no longer need for getting expensive skills, training employees, buying hardware, upgrading HW/SW every so often, deprecating or disposing the hardware. No more headaches.

SOA Applications layer virtualization

At the EA application layer, virtualization is provided by SOA through standard interfaces and encapsulation, hiding the implementation technology. More, SOA provides the standard integration technology with communications implemented over standard protocols and interfaces accessed in a standard manner.

SOA provides an abstraction layer above applications hiding the communications and applications implementation technology. It should not matter any longer how the applications and network are realized or what are the platforms. Applications are in effect virtualized and offered as services.

Inside the application layer, Java and .NET have already introduced a virtual machine abstraction layer between the applications and OS and Application Servers are providing even more abstracted functionality by adding distributed transactions, persistence, security and other horizontal capabilities.

The virtualization of the EA business layer design

At the EA business layer, workflows would be implemented by process and rules engines as orchestration of SOA and Web Services listed and described in a catalogue (UDDI, WSDL).

This abstracts away the complexity of IT and its applications under a layer which business people can understand and now model themselves. They would be able to design and change processes using BPEL (Business Process Execution Language), as a composition of SOA and SaaS business services, using graphical interfaces.

The virtualization of Information layer -MDM

For the EA information layer, MDM (Master Data Management) adds a similar virtualization layer since most application will utilize now information provided by this layer rather than supplied by all other applications. The MDM implementation may be integrated to SOA since the MDM hub could become a SOA service for information access. This will constitute a data abstraction layer for services and people using the information.

The virtualization of the User Interface

From a User Interface point of view, the fine grained Web2.0 interactivity further abstracts IT technology from business logic by providing a universal, ubiquitous web client, independent of application and its implementation with the performance of client server applications. An abstraction layer is introduced which consists of web servers understanding AJAX, Adobe Flash and MS Silverlight like technologies.

Key findings

A Virtual Enterprise (VE), as defined here, is a company consisting of a majority of business functions outsourced in a BPO (Business Process Outsourcing) manner; nonetheless a governance corporate function should still exist to coordinate all other function activities and legally identify the Enterprise. The BPO outsources the business processes, the technology and people executing them, and as such all layers of an Enterprise Architecture.

IT virtualization appears at the interface between EA layers, at the same time.

At the EA business layer, the business process orchestration and rules engines provide to business people the tool to rapidly change the Enterprise workflows and rules without support from IT.

At the EA application layer, virtualization is provided by SOA through standard interfaces and encapsulation of application, hiding the implementation technology. More, SOA provides the standard service integration technology.

At the EA information layer, MDM (Master Data Management) adds a similar virtualization interface since most application would utilize the information provided by this layer rather than supplied by all other applications.

And IT infrastructure virtualization is adding an interface layer hiding the IT implementation complexity and enabling efficient management of the processing capacity, storage and networks bandwidth. The IT infrastructure becomes increasingly a "real time" on demand service.

Overall, the virtualization of IT provides technology services to business through defined interfaces which eliminate the nowadays tangled business-IT interaction and provide abstraction interfaces between the EA layers of the Enterprise. There are multiple vertical and horizontal dimensions to the Enterprise virtualization about to happen or happening, as in the picture.

So what

Companies could deploy a combination of outsourcing strategies and IT virtualization technologies:

- entirely outsourced business processes, including the people operating them, through Business Process Outsourcing
- applications outsourced to Software as a Service, SaaS providers (or ASPs) with own people operating the application
- managed services where only the managing of your Applications and Infrastructure is outsourced
- the whole IT infrastructure outsourced to dedicated data centres
- IT virtualization will be pursued at all layers (BP orchestration and rules, MDM information, SOA services and integration, IT infrastructure)

Enterprises will be consciously designed out of SOA and SaaS services.

The business would take charge of its business processes through direct orchestration of SOA and SaaS services and direct access to the business rules technology.

Liberated from supporting most Value Chain functions a company may focus on its business planning, investing and creative management activities. The company will be lean, composed of a mix of best of breed outsourced services.

Other companies in the virtual Value Chain will similarly focus on fewer value chain links where they specifically have a competitive advantage like cheap or qualified labour, for instance: manufacturing in China, IT in India, consumer products in Japan, design in Europe, R&D in the US...

The new Enterprise business model is based on collaboration, virtualization technologies and outsourcing of links in the Value Chain.

The Cloud Enterprise

Business Process Utility, the Virtual Enterprise, Cloud Computing, Enterprise Architecture, SOA, all these business and IT developments – how could they all be deployed and integrated in a company? How would the concepts fit together and what would the outcome look like? There is so much confusion, particularly with IT concepts and technologies coming faster than we can absorb them, it is difficult to understand their consequences and their positioning next to each other.

The suggestion here is that a company developed according to these concepts would look like a Cloud Enterprise, that is, a Virtual Enterprise with a SOA-like architecture, with its business functions, processes, and their IT resources supplied over the Web by a cloud of business and IT service providers. The cloud symbol, coming from the networking world and, recently, Cloud Computing, signifies the Internet like distribution.

The Virtual Enterprise, described by some in the business field as the networked Enterprise, consists of transparently distributed business functions outsourced to partners that work together to deliver the product to the end customers. The Web and B2B have an important role in enabling this networked Enterprise. While not going into details, the essential benefit will be business agility and proficiency of the best of breed services.

'Business Process Utilities - BPU - are an emerging form of business process outsourcing. ABPU is useful when a more standardized solution is sought that can be paid for on a transactional basis" (Gartner, http://www.gartner.com/DisplayDocument?id=527120).

A classic example would be the personal credit verification, outsourced to specialized companies. Insurance is another domain where BPU registered progress. BPU may well extend to an entire business function, not just a process, as is often the case for HR or payroll. The technology supporting the process or function is outsourced with the function. What is new to BPU, as opposed to the traditional Business Process Outsourcing (BPO), is the fact that the service is rather standard, delivered to more than one customer and easy to integrate. BPU, in effect, supplies a process with an on demand consumption and charging model.

A Virtual Enterprise may, consist of a number of Business Processes Utilities or Functions outsourced to various provider firms.

Cloud Computing (CC) is a new overloaded IT term, and vague at that. In short, I would define it as the outsourcing of the IT services - applications and technology - to partners over the Web. Remote access or managed services relay an incomplete description since they suggest mostly people access. The cloud means outsourced applications integration and on demand, utility-like, services consumption, the novel elements of the model.

Cloud Computing represents, in fact, a new Enterprise business model where the IT services supporting the business are provided, to various degrees, by partners, rather than in-house. It sprang from IT, but so did SOA and Enterprise Architecture. The Cloud only refers to the services cloud of a single Enterprise. Every firm may have its own cloud that may overlap at multi-tenant IT service providers.

Cloud Computing consists of a few component service concepts (types of outsourced services): SaaS, PaaS (overall, I'll call them XaaS: Application, Platform, Infrastructure, Security... as a Service).

PaaS (Platform) and all its variants, as part of the Computing Cloud, offer the opportunity to outsource not only your data centre but to act as platforms for your applications, Web presence, content management... Integration as a Service emerges to provide the orchestration and integration of the XaaS services.

Because of the potential cocktails of various XaaS services, a few business models are possible. At one end, your applications may be outsourced to different SaaS providers in the Cloud, each using their own technology infrastructure. At the other end, the applications are housed by an Infrastructure/Data

Centre provider, or more than one, managed by a 3rd party. The applications may be owned and managed by the core firm or the application provider.

The Business Process Utility (BPU) business concept aligns well with the SaaS IT application service outsourcing even though BPU, in general, may not rely on IT. But, in reality, SaaS becomes a part of BPU. The difference is that one is an IT term while the other is business. They both are consumed and paid for on an "on demand" model.

Is the Cloud Computing (CC) a technology? To start with, it is the business concept of outsourcing IT services, really. As with SOA, companies such as Amazon, Google, Salesforce.com, Microsoft. and many others provide various CC models. From a supplier's perspective, the technology offered is sometimes called "private clouds," even if they are not really clouds that until they are included in an Enterprise cloud. A number of these private clouds may become part of an Enterprise cloud. And then for some, private cloud means own computing clouds which negate in fact the concept definition. But, in most cases, there still remain in-house applications, which have to interact with the cloud.

Among the benefits of the CC are instant provisioning of IT capabilities (servers, storage, network), utilization of the IT resources on demand (utility-like), service location independence (in the cloud, and technology transparency. The main advantage is that the service aims to be Off-the-Shelf, hiding the technology hurdles and fast and easy to adopt.

Among drawbacks are migration to the CC architecture, integration with other applications, and ownership of Enterprise data. Tools evolve to deploy/migrate applications transparently to different "private cloud" providers. Data security and legalities are key but not unsolvable. One has to separate data management from ownership. SOA, as a style, underlies the architecture of the services cloud.

A cloud computing paradigm, in actual fact, reduces an IT department in time to the IT architecture, strategy, and planning functions. The bitter relations of the past between IT and business could vanish, now replaced by contracts or real-time pre-pay for on demand services. Technology maintenance, upgrades, application management, and licenses are not your concern any longer.

The IT applications and technology become part of an Enterprise cloud. What does it mean? In

truth, gradually (as you deploy to the cloud), the IT becomes a separate entity from your Enterprise. Your applications may run in another time zone, country, and company. Along with the supporting IT applications, Business Processes are outsourced to partner companies, all part of an Enterprise Cloud now. And that leads us to Business Process Utility, facilitated by Cloud Computing.

CC demands technology Virtualization, without which it would be impossible for a provider to manage effectively the infrastructure serving many customers. It also stimulates the blades technology because of its scalability and reduced power consumption, etc.

The Cloud Computing directly affects the Enterprise Architecture; SOA offers transparent distribution, loose coupling, technology transparency, and interfaces rendering the integration light, so you can easily take full advantage of what the cloud offers. SOA, is essential in enabling the Virtual Enterprise, Cloud Computing, and Business Process Utility.

The cloud covers both the IT applications and technology layers of an Enterprise Architecture. Imagine the EA Business Architecture layer resting on top of the IT Application and Technology layers, as in the text book, now looking like a fluffy cloud of distributed, outsourced IT services.

The firm needs to draw the overall Enterprise Architecture, but not bother with the technological detail any longer. The Data Centre and its Virtualization, Grid computing, and blades technologies become less a concern for the business at large but more for the private clouds providers.

There is synergy between the Cloud Computing IT view (based on SaaS, PaaS, IaaS) the Virtual Enterprise business view and outsourced Business Process Utilities. All outsource functionality, eventually over the Internet. All become part of the cloud. All are best served by SOA. Ultimately, the

Cloud Computing serves and becomes part of the Virtual Enterprise or, if in need of a common term, the Cloud Enterprise.

The problem appears to be that business has a different language and vocabulary from IT. There is a deep division between business and IT in terms of skills and goals. The news is that Cloud Computing, supported by SOA, may bridge the division by outsourcing IT services to various service provider firms under SLA contracts.

The Cloud Enterprise has the agility of SOA and the low cost, convenience, and proficiency of Cloud Computing and Business Process Utility outsourcing, while taking advantage of the current networking and Internet capabilities.

While the EAI integrated the IT applications of yesterday, and the ESB serves the today's paradigm, the Web will integrate the largely distributed Cloud Enterprises of tomorrow, structured on SOA.

In a simple picture, the Cloud Enterprise looks like a cloud of business and IT service providers surrounding and serving a core firm. In a more complex view, Enterprises, consisting of core firms, collaborate with service provider firms, which, in turn, work with other service providers in their cloud to deliver the goods. It all comes down to Porter's Value systems – that is, a number of company Value Chains that are collaborating to deliver the end products.

The Digital Enterprise of the future

While, at first sight, it looks like "digital" is much ado about nothing, the sheer multitude, size and rapid progress, accumulation and penetration of digital technologies in the enterprise accelerates the urgency of the issue. Enterprise may be wasted over night because of the fast evolution of digital. Take, for instance, Nokia.

Businesses have suddenly woken up to the realisation that the world goes rapidly digital and that the conventional management may not be able to lead on this path. To succeed, new competencies are needed such as a wide technology command and a comprehension of the impact on the enterprise. Pundits have already embarked in campaigns of the kind "do digital or die". Right, but how would a digital enterprise look like?

But, businesses existed for hundreds of years before the "digital" technology was born. Then, why should we do it, only because some say so?

In any case, the digital technologies evolution or perhaps, revolution, is on our cards for the long run. It is an ever on-going process. We just have to drive the enterprise on the right digital path, that is to make best use of digital developments. Because our competitors would do exactly that.

The evolution to Digital is not an option but a "must". While we are already doing it, we have to prepare for the increasingly accelerated rate of Digital progress. With the acceleration of Digital progress, the enterprise technology landscape changes faster than ever. Networks, disks, storage and processors grow more powerful, faster and cheaper. Information storage capacity soars at an unprecedented pace.

The digital enterprise stems from the convergence of online marketing and sales, social networking technologies, mobility, process automation and orchestration, virtualisation of computing, the cloud (SaaS, IaaS, PaaS...), big data analytics, internet of things and many other. How to make best use of them is the question.

The Digital Technologies impact on the Enterprise

- Virtualisation enables the separation of applications, processing, storage and network entities from the physical hardware, enabling as such easy online resource creation, configuration, scalability, availability, portability... and, hence, business operation agility.
- In-memory databases enable instant processing and real time analytics.
- Applications such as Portals, Information and Document Management, Access Control, Enterprise Orchestration and Integration Buses, CRM, Call Centres, ERPs - Finance, HR, Procurement...- are increasingly automating off-the-shelf the enterprise.
- Web powerful standard interactive technologies based on UI languages like HTML5 and scripting
- Mobile technology ensure fast access to the enterprise information and applications
- Social Media facilitates bi-directional contact with customers.
- Open source technology opens up cheaper IT avenues.
- Robotics, automated production bands
- Tele-collaboration and conferencing technologies
- Electronic B2B transactions with partners and suppliers
- Customer Data Integration (CDI) and Master Data Management (MDM)
- Big Data, advanced business intelligence for Decision support
- Business applications and flows Integration based on business rules
- On-line sales, payment

- AI, Virtual reality, 3D printing, Internet of Things, self driving cars, robots, transport drones

And ultimately, enabled by the Digital progress, the Cloud changes the paradigm of IT ownership. The IT goes back to the shared data centre. We rent from the data centre processing power, storage and networking rather than buy, maintain, upgrade, discard and recycle.

Paradoxically, the Cloud, by outsourcing the IT services over the net, offers us a degree of insulation from the digital technology rapid evolution. We don't have to master the IT any longer.

In fact, the Cloud makes our digital evolution easier. Because we manage our business functions and processes independent of technology and its location.

But why would the business care about Digital at all?

Because of the impact of Digital on the business operation: faster responses, more intuitive UIs, more agile configurations able to respond to market changes, more scalability, more integration of processes, information and technology, more off-the-shelf choices, more automation... more of everything.

In the Digital era, the enterprise would be increasingly distributed, interconnected and automated. Many new small enterprises would be part of the enterprise virtual value chain in an interconnected economy. The enterprise would be agile, faster to market, leaner and meaner.

The integration of data, the user experience and the quality of intelligence would be progressively better.

Customers would benefit from better and new types of products, all digitally enhanced.

All technologies, capabilities and products would be enhanced by Digital technology. That would pave the way to the Internet of Things (IoT), that is Things that co-operate to deliver a service.

The Digital evolution would affect the way we do business and the organisation of the enterprise.

We must prepare the enterprise to evolve towards a virtual enterprise, enabled by Digital technology, where various business processes and services are/maybe outsourced to partners in the Cloud world in various business models.

The Digital transforms as such the way our enterprises are created and operate. Companies in partnership, collaborating to deliver a product, act as the value chain links of an overall virtual enterprise composed of many small and distributed enterprises. The name of the game is cooperation.

The Digital technology would create many new products and services.

The Digital would enable innovation and invention in many sectors.

To survive in the digital enterprise space, the management needs to understand how all these technologies affect the enterprise and how do they work together to serve a customer that already lives in a world of digital entertainment, on-line purchasing, personal cloud services... and digital gadgets.

How would the digital enterprise ultimately look like?

In this vision, the enterprise could be

- Virtual, stretching over the boundaries of a few physical enterprises owing to the Cloud and business process outsourcing enabled by fast digital communications, collaboration, B2B and transport technologies
- Increasingly Lego like, assembled from parts such as SaaS services that would be remotely plugged in and out and configured, scaled... over the net.
- The new paradigm would be leasing capabilities/outsourcing rather than buying and owning them.
- Automated end to end, with applications covering all enterprise functions and workflows and transactions executed without manual intervention due to the increasingly expanding

application suites, services, IOT... beside robots, assembly bands

- Smaller office footprints due to remote working, mobile access and ubiquitous communication technologies
- On-line sales, payment, marketing and customer interaction based on web social media technologies
- Virtual shops manned by virtual reality technologies, decreasing physical shop footprint
- Information, integrated, normalised, consistent... due to MDM, CDI, integrated application suites...
- Real time business intelligence, due to in-memory platforms
- On-the-net data store and back-up on the Cloud

To cope, it is important to comprehend our own enterprise better, its the structure and operation so that we can factor the Digital in a quick and safe manner.

We have to be good at evaluating the technologies that are about to change the enterprise.

We have to include the Digital in our Strategy and planning.

But we have to control the Digital evolution rather that the vice versa.

Adopting a technology frantically, one at a time, without the benefit of the big picture, may ultimately contribute to failure rather than success.

Can the current IT though handle the massive digitisation of the enterprise at such a rate?

It is hard, if not impossible to consider all technologies and trends and then make sense and understand impacts in the context of your enterprise. But someone in the enterprise has to do it in a structured manner.

More often than not though, the traditional CIO and IT department are not part of the solution space at least because their legacy is to keep the IT alive rather than watch the evolution of all the technology landscape.

The Enterprise Modelling though is the first step in the transformation to Digital.

The Enterprise Modeller job is not only has to discover and document the enterprise structure and operation but has to align technologies to the business mission and vision so that the strategy is achieved.

To simplify the landscape the digital architect has to also virtualise and separate the layers of the enterprise IT. See "The Virtualisation of the Enterprise".

Hence, today, the Enterprise Modeller is well positioned to establish the digital enterprise vision and coordinate the transformation to achieve it.

But the right architects have to be raised to the level where they have a mandate to do the job.

A checklist for a successful transformation

One has to make sure that:

- the leadership is properly chosen on professional rather than political criteria, so that is aware of the business problem and company culture while understands the technical solution
- the transformation process
  - consists of stand alone phases and projects, with Go/No-Go milestones and criteria, so that the process can be adjusted or stopped as necessary to limit losses when risks materialise
  - is agile enough to take into account new dependencies and requirements
  - is risk tolerant in that risks are continually evaluated and the associated contingency plans are in place since start
- the transformation governance ensures that:

- o authority comes with accountability
- o principles, guidelines, policies and roadmaps are in place to guide the decision making and makers
- o the experts are empowered to make decisions rather than the committees and administrators even though these should be consulted
- o problem evaluation and solution design are double checked by a third party
- o the problem is analysed and the solution designed in the Enterprise Architecture context.
- o The EA blueprint should be available before the transformation starts rather than modelled at the same time
- o a staging platform is created before changes go live in order to avoid business malfunctions, dissatisfaction and operating losses
- o change roll back is embedded in procedure and planning.
- o Recording change history, to find out, where and what things went wrong, is a must.
- o before the transformation, antidotes for the existing poor enterprise practices and culture are embedded in process and practices
- o Communications with stakeholders and enterprise employees is adequately performed to advertise events, poll support and feedback is received and acted upon.
- o Security, backup, scalability, availability, systems management... are considered in the transformation right from the beginning

While in every day operation the lack of proper management practices is easy to conceal, these practices however would most likely fail the next large company transformation.

It was found though that in many approaches there is made little distinction between capabilities, processes and flows. That makes them hard to use in Enterprise Architecture modelling since there is no distinction between structure and behaviour. You may easily discover that the taxonomy used in these various frameworks will rarely map on your organization and even less on your technology architecture. These frameworks can be hardly used for EA design. Most of the time they are process taxonomies of various kinds.

Also most approaches cannot be represented as architecture, even though they are shown in boxes sometimes, since they do not consist of components in interconnections.

The Digital Transformation should rely on Enterprise Architecture

Key Points:

o Our life has already been digitised
o The digital enterprise is inevitable
o Why do we care about digital
o The digital developments that affect your enterprise
o The impact of Digital on business models and value chains
o How would the end game digital enterprise look like from a business angle
o Benefits of the digital enterprise
o How to prepare the enterprise
o Is today's Enterprise Architecture adequate enough though to guide the enterprise to the future?
o The Enterprise Modelling approach
o The digital road is never ending

What is the digital technology?

It all starts from the transformation of information and analogue signals into a digital representation of 0/1s. Complicated mathematical algorithms in software can then process the information. General or special purpose computers and microprocessors host the information processing. The faster and smaller the hardware, the more capable is our digital world.

Our life has already been digitised

Our watches, media, players, phones, tablets, GPSs, laptops, radios, TVs, ... are all digital. All networks and transmissions are digital, our pets are micro-chipped, our cars are increasingly computerised..., we are equipped with digital pacemakers and hearing aids. We have complex digital instruments, airplanes and weapons.

The digitisation of the enterprise, do we have to worry about it?

Everybody talks about digitisation of the enterprise today. Pundits make their business in alerting us that digital is coming like a storm, that we have to do something about it. We had technology since the first enterprise though. Did we have to worry about it? Not really, not more than necessary. Because it is the normal course of things.

Still, the first to have a better tool or weapon has a decisive advantage.

The first enterprise to have an effective technology would have a competitive advantage. The enterprises that choose and properly integrate the increasing plethora of technologies will win.

Because digitisation happens since long then, what's different now?

Change took a long time in the past. In the 1950s we had the first TVs and computers. But technology evolved so much that a mobile phone today has many times the power of the first computer. The hardware that occupied rooms now is hosted in a bankcard chip or SIM.

According to Ray Kurzweil, "technological change is exponential, contrary to the common-sense "intuitive linear" view. So we won't experience 100 years of progress in the 21st century — it will be more like 20,000 years of progress (at today's rate). We're doubling the rate of progress every decade"

Hence, it is not so much the digitisation of the enterprise but its acceleration.

And it is the Moore's Law that explains the Digital revolution. It states that processing power doubles every two years or so. Thus, computers have increasingly the capacity to execute in real time the complex algorithms we devised long time ago.

Why the digital enterprise is inevitable?

Do we have to take the digital enterprise path? Is it evitable? What would be the advantages?

The digital enterprise is happening nolens volens, that is, there is no choice. The enterprise cannot really escape the technology progress.

We cannot avoid the digital revolution. And it is a revolution indeed, because the change is significantly larger now and faster gathering pace and accumulating change. Moreover, we are already engaged on the digital path.

Even though the digital future is inevitable, we can still make choices and actively control the digital evolution from as early as possible to get what we want, in accord with our vision, rather than accept what comes.

But why do we care about digital?

And why should we do it, only because some say so? Businesses existed for hundreds of years before the "digital" technology was born.

But technology progress and in particular, the Digital pace that fuels it, is, perhaps, the biggest factor of change but also opportunities and threats in the enterprise and elsewhere today.

The Digital progress enables smaller size, larger scale, more amiable User Interfaces, faster processing and communications, increasing automation and integration of processes, information and technology and on a business level, new products, business models and organisation k9nds, i.e. more of everything.

But we have to control the Digital evolution rather that the vice versa.

Adopting a technology frantically, one at a time, without the benefit of the big picture, may ultimately contribute to failure rather than success. Still, there are many more and more to come.

The digital developments that affect your enterprise

With the acceleration of Digital progress, the enterprise technology landscape changes faster and faster.

- Networks, disks, storage and processors grow more powerful, faster and cheaper
- Information storage capacity soars at an unprecedented pace
- Virtualisation enables the separation of applications, processing, storage and network entities from the physical hardware, enabling as such easy online resource creation, configuration, scalability, availability, portability... and, hence, business operation agility.
- In-memory databases enable instant processing and real time analytics.
- Open Source enables increasingly affordable, cost effective applications
- Application suites, increasingly expanding to automate the whole enterprise operation, such as Portals, Information and Document Management, Access Control, Orchestration and Enterprise Integration Buses, CRM, ERPs
- The Web added powerful standard user interaction technologies based on UI languages like HTML5 and Java scripting
- Mobile access ensures fast access to the enterprise functions from anywhere, on the go.
- Social Media facilitates bi-directional contact with customers and prospects
- Tele-collaboration and conferencing technologies replace travelling
- Electronic B2B transactions with partners and suppliers reduce transaction and face to face time

- Customer Data Integration (CDI) and Master Data Management (MDM) that reduce your data integrity issues
- Big Data business intelligence facilitate Decision making
- Virtual reality enable shops
- 3D printing and robots ease manufacturing
- Internet of Things enable context reactive operations
- Self driving cars and drones reduce transport costs
- And, not least, enabled by the Digital progress, the Cloud changes the paradigm of IT ownership. The IT goes back to the shared data centre. We rent from the data centre processing power, storage and networking and application rather than buy, maintain, upgrade, discard and recycle our own.

The impact of Digital on business models and value chains

The progress of Digital technology brings in the enterprise new business models.

Companies increasingly market, sale and service over net channels, rent their resources from the cloud and let partners provide the processing links of the enterprise value chain. Take the example of so many firms today that outsource manufacturing, sales, marketing or, on the other hand, the product design and development, with most of them outsourcing now the enterprise support functions.

But customer channels, resources and partners are the key elements of any business model.

New companies appear, mainly comprising of management staff who assemble the pieces of the business from services that execute the links of the value chain, from sourcing to making and delivery over various channels.

The companies may just have a web site, hosted and designed by somebody else at that. But, the enterprise still owns the product and manages the whole production chain.

The new business model is of the "virtual value chain" kind. Both business processes and technology are outsourced to partners and cloud providers. The Digital progress supplies the integration network, the virtualisation base, the off-the-shelf Cloud services, the customer channels... that ultimately automate the virtual value chain.

The enterprise creation becomes a matter of integrating the partner services and the Cloud infrastructure that deliver the value chain the entrepreneur establishes. Everything is rented.

The cost of both failure and success is much smaller as such.

The only function that remains in the physical enterprise is the management that selects, configures and coordinates the links of the virtual value chain.

This function will also identify the enterprise.

The Digital transforms as such the way our enterprises are created and operate.

Companies in partnership, collaborating to deliver a product, act as the value chain links of an overall virtual enterprise composed of many small and distributed enterprises.

The name of the game is cooperation.

Without the Digital technology progress, that would not have been possible.

The Digital evolution affects as such the way we do business and the organisation of the enterprise which would evolve towards a virtual organisation enabled by Digital technology where various business processes and services are/maybe outsourced to partners in the Cloud world in various business models.

The enterprise would be increasingly distributed, interconnected and automated. Many new small enterprises would be part of the enterprise virtual value chain in an interconnected economy.

How would the end game digital enterprise look like from a business angle

Pundits have already embarked in campaigns of the kind "do digital or die". Right, but how would a digital business look like?

But indeed, the user experience and the quality of intelligence would be progressively better. Customers would benefit from better and new types of products, all digitally enhanced.

In this vision, the enterprise could be:

Virtual

stretching over the boundaries of a few physical enterprises owing to the Cloud and business process outsourcing enabled by fast digital communications, collaboration, B2B and transport technologies

Increasingly Lego like

assembled from parts such as SaaS services that would be remotely plugged in and out and configured, scaled... over the net.

Leasing capabilities

rather than buying and owning them.

Automated

end to end, with applications covering all enterprise functions and workflows and transactions executed without manual intervention due to the increasingly expanding application suites, services, IOT... beside robots, assembly bands

Small office footprint

due to remote working, mobile access and ubiquitous communication technologies

On-line sales, payment...,

marketing and customer interaction based on web social media technologies

Virtual shops

manned by virtual reality technologies, decreasing physical shop footprint

Information, integrated, normalised, consistent...

due to MDM, CDI, integrated application suites...

Real time business intelligence

due to in-memory platforms

On-the-net data store

and back-up on the Cloud

Benefits of the digital enterprise

All technologies, capabilities and products would be enhanced by Digital technology. That would pave the way to the Internet of Things (IoT), that is Things that co-operate to deliver a service.

Also, the Digital gradually renders the enterprise virtual with most parts residing in a cloud of partners that participate into the Value Chain. What matters most and identifies the enterprise is the Governance function that coordinates the enterprise Operations, Development and Support activities that can and are increasingly outsourced. See "The Cloud Enterprise".

The Digital would enable the enterprise and its stakeholders benefit in many ways. The digital revolution will enable

The business be in control of the enterprise operation and evolution since capabilities will be purchased and configured on-line by the business and mounted only for the required period

- The Designed Enterprise, that is, a business architected from parts or services from the Cloud and Business Process Outsourcing (BPO) providers

- The business will select capabilities rather than the IT
- More reliable planning and predictable costs owing to the availability of readymade capabilities, rather than relying on building in-house
- Technology expertise to be relegated to service provider firms rather than to each and every enterprise
- Quick scalability, configurability, reporting... agility to change, features inherited from capabilities
- Instant decision making based on Real Time Business Intelligence
- Model Driven Manufacturing where the design to manufacturing process is automated with 3D printing
- Drones enabled distribution

Technology evolution would enable Business to be in control of the enterprise rather than continue to tinker with technology like today.

The enterprise, overall, would be more agile, faster to market as such, leaner and meaner.

How to prepare the enterprise

Digital, perhaps, is the biggest factor of change in the enterprise or elsewhere today. It abounds in opportunities but it is also a threat for the complacent enterprise. But the Digital quandary consists not only in what are the right technologies for our enterprise but how are we going to integrate them into the enterprise and when. This is compounded by the fact that the Digital progress accelerates. And more technology like the Cloud move technology ownership and management outside the enterprise.

But to ensure our enterprise succeeds in a digital future, we have to understand first the technology impacts and trends. Then, we have to be good at evaluating the technologies that are about to change the enterprise.

What do we need to do in practice?

The Digital technology would create many new products and services. Think about them early.

The Digital would enable innovation and invention in many sectors. Reflect on that.

We have to include the Digital in our Strategy and planning.

To cope, it is important to comprehend our own enterprise better, its the structure and operation so that we can factor the Digital in a quick and safe manner.

To mitigate the threats of the future, we need to project now the enterprise picture in a few years time. We need to think strategically. And then we need to prepare the enterprise for the accelerating pace of change.

Hence, it's a good practice to create a function in the enterprise that focuses on the enterprise future.

Enterprise Architecture already discovers, documents the enterprise and projects its future states but only from an IT perspective.

Is today's EA adequate enough to guide the enterprise to the future?

In theory, EA does enable the enterprise transformation, the same way the blueprint of your house or town enables change. Without a blueprint, laying cables in the wall or under the pavement is a risky endeavour because you may break the existing electricity wires and water or gas pipes. In practice though, few EA efforts deliver the EA blueprint and as such, EA enables neither change nor transformation today.

Anyway, EA does not deliver business benefits directly. The business itself must transform the enterprise, employing EA, to reduce duplication in processes, platforms, projects, to streamline the operation, fix malfunctions, map strategy, project the future etc. The architect should deliver the "big picture", propose changes and assist. Without delivering the big picture, EA fails after all.

The paradox today is that while there are plenty of EA architects, there are few Enterprise Architectures. That means that architects do not deliver EA but rather stories about it and engage in never ending efforts and self important discourses. Most architects sell again and again the EA known benefits rather than do EA.

Anyway, business stakeholders don't know what to expect or, if they know, thinking by analogy of an architecture blueprint, they are quite pessimistic about it, noting the disaccord between promises and results in practice. For most, EA is potentially costly and largely, prone to fail.

The subsequent paradox is that even if EA does not deliver, business customers do not complain because, for most, despite the propaganda, EA is still an internal IT effort of little consequence to the wider enterprise.

In any case, it is not so much the architect but the architecture itself and principles that matter to a transformation and the end system. As with a building, the blueprint is what matters after the original architect is long gone.

The Enterprise Modelling approach

We need an approach that focuses on the enterprise as a whole, its change and the transition to that state but also to prepare the enterprise for disruption.

What the Function has to do though before even looking at incoming change is to

1. understand better and describe the operation and capabilities of the current enterprise

2. prepare a technology obsolescence roadmap to enable a natural evolution

3. architect the enterprise for future change, for flexibility and agility to move on, so that it can be easily and quickly configured out of modules, ready made services that can be filled in by best of breed.

That is, you have to model the enterprise to be able to visualise it, enable the enterprise self awareness and the projection of the target picture.

But, ironically, the digital revolution gradually removes the IT as an enterprise concern by moving it back to the Cloud. The Computing Cloud is, in fact, an IT technology, that gradually renders the enterprise technology agnostic.

Hence, an enterprise function, beyond the IT Enterprise Architecture, i.e. current EA, will have to discover the existing business and organizational landscape and architect it

- resources agnostic because the technology and/or people may be supplied by 3rd parties
- ownership agnostic, after all, most capabilities can be outsourced for execution by 3rd parties
- service based, that is, the key role is occupied by the interface protocols and APIs
- integrates Information and people organisation architecture

We are looking then at an **Enterprise Modelling** function, rather than EA, that should be in charge of the end to end Enterprise discovery and modelling besides the trends and emerging technologies integration and roadmapping.

The function would be operating at the top management level rather than IT.

And indeed the Enterprise Modelling function has to

- liaise with functions to understand business and technology needs
- analyse the evolving and new trends and technologies potential impact on the business
- merge technology evolution into the overall enterprise strategy
- architect technologies integration to functions without duplication or unnecessary variation or replacement
- establish the principles and standards of enterprise transformation

- produce the target enterprise blueprint
- propose a roadmap for discussion and approval
- facilitate the transformation process

TheDigital road ahead is never ending

The Digital road is long, without an end in site. In fact, we have already embarked on this road long ago.

Since it affects now the whole enterprise, technology becomes a key competitive differentiator. Hence, we have to prepare the enterprise for the digital road because technology could make or break the enterprise.

What do you do though to make sure your enterprise evolves on the right digital path? Digital adoption can be expensive or ineffective if not properly thought. Not all digital technologies, for instance, would be productive for your chosen evolution. And, without proper integration in your operations and vision, the digital can create an additional weight. Digital at all costs does not pay off.

To succeed in the digital transformation today, we have to project the big picture at the end of the tunnel, the digital enterprise, the same way we do in enterprise architecture.

You need a true and strong digital team that operates at top business level to cover the whole enterprise rather than IT alone because technology is in IT care because it implements the business functionality.

Yet, what we do today is embark in implementing the digital step by step, technology by technology. and hope for the best. Yet this path does not allow us to control the final outcome but strands of it.

What makes the difference is not so much the technologies employed but the degree of integration into your enterprise operation and vision so that technologies offer your maximum benefit at minimum cost and render the enterprise competitive.

The digital technologies may also transform your vision of the enterprise though and more, change its business models.

The paradox we live today is that the progress of IT leads increasingly to the outsourcing of the very technology that enables it. Perhaps because the effort to manage properly its increasing complexity becomes too costly and steals the focus of your enterprise. With the Cloud, the enterprise would own less and less technology.

The information technology is also increasingly hidden under virtualisation layers.

But virtualisation introduces a layer of abstraction that enables outsourcing. Note the growing reliance on processing, storage and network virtualisation and the services paradigm in software. See also "The Virtualization of the Enterprise".

In any case, the digital technologies evolution or perhaps, revolution, is on our cards for the long run. It is an ever on-going process. We just have to drive the enterprise on the right digital path, that is to make best use of digital developments because others would do exactly that.

The evolution to Digital is not an option but a "must". But while we are already doing it, we have to prepare for the increasingly accelerated rate of Digital progress.

Enterprise Architecture as Reference, Governance and Story for the Enterprise Transformation

EA as governance for the enterprise transformation

The EA group has to create a governance framework that would be employed in the consistent design of EA artefacts, solution architectures and EA decision making process.

All stakeholders have to conform with the EA governance. For instance, stakeholders should check the EA before any investment in their field to determine the components affected, the platforms recommended and similar technologies already available so that the investment attains is objectives without creating duplication or overlay in the process.

Because architectural debt is created if "projects make decisions in isolation.

The governance should act through established and widely approved principles, control checkpoints in processes and project phases, roadmaps, strategies and decision making policies that establish who makes what decisions on which parts... The governance should be agreed beforehand rather than being elaborated on the run, as it happens today. One has to make sure though that the governance has input and meets the approval of all concerned parts. Governance should be approved by a more encompassing and different body from EA so that project architects and many other stakeholders may have a say.

Then, projects and activities should all submit to the governing rules and body, which body may not necessarily be the EA group but may have participation from. The Governance should be constantly reviewed and updated.

Governance reduces chaos. Governance avoids friction. Governance enforces integration, consistency and predictable results.

EA as reference for the transformation

How do you design the target architecture if you do not discover and document first the architecture of what is out there? How could you expand a building without taking into account its current structure? You may end up transforming a barn in a concert hall.

In the absence of the current architecture, the enterprise may end up being re-designed from scratch at each cycle.

How could you plan a proper enterprise transformation if you do not know the current organisation and processes, the current systems and technologies, the as-is capabilities to act on their strengths and weaknesses?

How could you perform the gap analysis and establish the roadmap to the end state?

What would happen with the current platforms, skills and investments if you replace them when you ignore them starting from scratch?

How would the enterprise continue to deliver its products and pay your salary during such a transformation that may end up making you redundant?

The EA blueprint is about the current enterprise state. It enables the understanding, maintenance, fixing, improvement and transformation of the enterprise.

The enterprise evolves incrementally employing the existing processes and platforms rather than in revolutionary cycles. Even revolutions re-use existing structures.

Besides, a target enterprise that fails to consider the current operation and technologies would make your management cringe, to put it nicely. The transformation cost and risks would be insurmountable. Abandoning assets half way through their life cycle, unamortised yet, would waste investments. What would the shareholders and the investors say?

Too often though strategic transformations start, unfortunately without the architecture of the current enterprise. Too often the current EA is just embedded in people's minds. That increase the risks and costs of any transformation because nobody has the entire picture to make sure the transformation streams work towards that single goal. The current EA would make the transformation faster, cheaper, more effective, predictable and less riskier. The current enterprise architecture is a reference for the enterprise transformation because we refer to and transform what we have rather than building the enterprise from scratch.

EA as a story for transformation

So, where is the "story" idea coming from? To me the question is, are we turning our backs to "A picture says a thousand words"?

After all, EA is an architecture and the blueprint of the enterprise. At least, the words in the naming lead us to the logical conclusion that EA is a picture. And a building architecture is expressed in blueprints rather than stories, as we all know.

The story approach looks like springing from the popular tradition of employing plastic imagery, metaphors and comparisons to explain things in simple terms to people who have little patience, time and knowledge of the domain. And, at times, we may be all appreciating a well told simple story rather than the technical explanations.

It is also true that in recent times, even the professional literature is full of stories written in a colourful language rather than worded in the precise language of the profession.

A story may help stakeholders visualise how the enterprise will work after development. A story may come as a presentation to gain approval from the relevant stakeholders. The story is not used though to develop EA but to narrate the "change" for people to understand and subsequently approve it.

Anyway, it is not the EA architect that dictates the future state of the enterprise but the management, its vision and business strategy. Is it likely then that the strategy team puts together the story anyway.

What an EA architect has to accomplish then is to translate the story into use cases and target EA the that illustrate the impacts on processes, organisation, components and technologies of the enterprise.

The EA architect should devise the architecture that illustrates "how the new world would work" and the roadmap to show "what change would happen".

Nevertheless, should such a story be necessary, the teller function should be perhaps played by strategy and marketing teams. It is the marketing that usually illustrates how the "customer is made happy" for example.

Are we, the EA architects, in a position of command to tell stories and have the people listen? I doubt it. Would the management even expect the EA architect come with tales instead of pictures and roadmaps?

Ultimately, it is true that we have to "sell" the EA results as best as we can, by telling stories, if necessary. But that's not part of the EA development or utilisation process. Anyway, the architects have to be fluent in explaining the impacts of EA, stories or not. They should be indeed good communicators.

To conclude, stories may help certain audiences understand change by employing common language and light narrative. But stories are not how EA is done or represented though.

The Digital Transformation for the Executive Lot

The Digital is a transformation all enterprises have to go through. Even if it does not really guarantee the success of your enterprise, it is nevertheless a condition for your enterprise survival. Because your enterprise must automate to reduce costs, employ IOT and Edge Computing to enhance operation, enable real time decisions by AI and be accessible online for transactions, exchanges and information... Because most business changes today are induced by technology whose renewal cycles get shorter and shorter. Hence, from now on, we are stuck with the Digital.

As a note though, the more Digital the enterprise becomes the less it cares about the Digital because the Digital increasingly enables the outsourcing of IT to the Cloud which offers on demand pools of functionality, processing power, edge computing, storage and networking. Hence, paradoxically, with the Digital Transformation the IT will continue to slide out of the enterprise into the Cloud. The more Cloud there is, the less Digital is the enterprise. But "Why So Many High-Profile Digital Transformations Fail" ?

Thomas H. Davenport analyses in this article for Harvard Business Review a few digital transformations attempt: "Procter & Gamble wanted to become "the most digital company on the planet"... It happened with analytics and big data... And now it's happening with digital transformation..."

To start with this failures are no big cause of alarm. When 70% of all IT projects fail anyhow, no wonder Digital Transformations fail. The situation is bad but no worse than usual. Yet, we should learn how to prevent these failures.

After talking through the few culprit reasons, Thomas notes that a cause of failure is digital transformations "decisions are inevitably influenced by hype from vendors and the media, expensive consultants offering "thought leadership" insights, many high profile experiments, and a few exciting success stories...".

True, today even the academy and business consulting firms like HBR, Boston Consulting, McKinsey, Forbes, ... which kept for so long their distance from IT, are all into Digital telling us incessantly what we have to do to save our enterprise from the assault of the Digital technology. They are even into Enterprise Architecture (EA) today, which was so IT that they wouldn't touch with a pole. It is true that, from the beginning the Digital Transformation was touted by self promoting prophets who worked on the assumption that if it happens they can claim the "I-said-so" and if it doesn't, nobody would cares anyway. Yet, this hype is pretty much the case for any new development today. So this reason for failure is so common that it does not make any difference in fact.

Davenport also writes that the lesson learned by P&G is that "no digital initiative is undertaken at P&G if it doesn't fit the strategy closely and if it's not hardwired to value".

It is politically correct to say that, but is it right? The IT guys know well today that digital initiatives cannot be always hardwired to value but rather to the total cost of doing business as usual because, for instance, they often have to upgrade a technology at a considerable effort and cost only because the suppliers support no longer the current versions.

Still, what is the root cause of the Digital Transformation failures?

The root cause of failure is that the Digital Transformation is performed in a single step as, a one off, big sudden transformation that not only disrupts the business as usual but has a very good chance to fail due to its high ambitions.

The Digital transformation (DT) has been already happening for a long time now, beginning, arguably, with the introduction of computers in the enterprise. Further more, the digital technologies would not stop evolving over night, but, on the contrary, the pace of change will accelerate. In fact, the Digital Transformation came to our attention again only when this pace of change has began to overwhelm the enterprise. In fact, in what we are concerned today, the pace of updates of the Windows OS and Android transforms us all nervous wrecks.

As such, the Digital is a single continuous and ever faster transformation rather than a one-off transformation as touted today. A Digital Transformation would be followed by yet another and another.

How should we prevent the failure of our Digital Transformation?

To succeed, the enterprise must go first through a few preparatory changes enumerated below in order to ease the incoming Digital Transformation per se, changes that would render the enterprise agile to the incoming change. Without these preparatory steps the Digital Transformation may fail when your enterprise architecture looks like a hair ball which you would have to untangle late, during the transformation.

But here are the preparatory steps:

1. Model the current Architecture of the Enterprise so that you evaluate

a). the enterprise landscape at the start of your transformation

b). the architecture end state and the changes that need to be done to render the enterprise agile to all the incoming digital change

In this phase you document the current enterprise model, establish the architecture principles for the transformation and model the enterprise end picture according to them. This way, you clean-up your enterprise architecture and pay the enterprise architectural debt to prevent the many future failures that may spring due to poor documentation and the short cuts taken in the past.

For agility, organise as much as possible the target enterprise architecture around services so that you are able to control all dependencies and enable outsourcing. As such encapsulate services, define APIs, microservices... Plan potential outsourcing from the very beginning to be able to work with suppliers.

The outcome of this work would be the

- Newly created Enterprise Modelling team, if you don't already have one
- Current Enterprise Architecture documented from the Process, Technology and People Organisation points of view
- Architecturally correct, debt free target Enterprise Architecture documented in terms of Process, Technology and People
- Workstreams and milestones to achieve the target enterprise architecture

2. Document in parallel with 1.) the relevant Emerging Technologies landscape

Without a thorough effort to evaluate the potential digital technologies you may miss those developments that render your enterprise competitive.

Outcomes:

- A newly established Emerging Technology team
- A Digital Strategy and Roadmap including the key relevant technologies, dependencies and the milestones of adoption

3. Establish the Digital Transformation Plan and a long term Roadmap

because, no matter how good it sounds, no enterprise would engage in separate pre-transformations for the sake of the Enterprise Modelling or Agility alone.

The Strategy and Planning teams, working with the EA and Emerging Technologies deliver:

- A single overall Enterprise Strategy that includes the Business, Digital and Architecturally correct strategies

- The short term Enterprise Transformation plan and the long term Roadmap which implement the Business vision, Digital technologies and Architecture Principles all in one

Proceed with the execution of the single continuous Transformation Plan in iterations, while refreshing, as you go, the roadmap.

The Enterprise Architect Role

The enterprise must change rapidly today to cope with the accelerating market and technology evolution. Since at any one time change is happening in the enterprise in one form or another, the enterprise changes continuously today.

When major change is necessary the enterprise should adopt a transformation process in order to coordinate all change of the enterprise under the same umbrella and attempt to minimise disruption and down time.

Yet, if you don't understand your enterprise you cannot change it properly, not in any case without major additional costs, setbacks, delays and expensive downtime.

For stakeholders to grasp the complexities of the enterprise in the same way though you need to model your enterprise so that everyone visualises and discusses solutions on the same picture. The outcome is indeed the enterprise schematics or otherwise called Enterprise Architecture (EA).

The reasons Enterprise Architecture (EA) is necessary today are many fold

In the first place you need the EA so that anyone in the enterprise can understand it in order to operate it collectively at its optimum.

On the other hand you must have the enterprise schematics to be able to divide and conquer and in general manage the increasing complexity of the enterprise today.

And in the end, since without EA change or transformation regularly fails, you do Enterprise Architecture to model the impact of change on the entire enterprise from the very beginning so that you act on all dependencies and effect their change in sync rather than on the run with holdbacks and late discoveries.

The Enterprise Modeller is naturally the Enterprise Architect (EA), the leader of the EA development effort and the owner of the EA framework which lays out the EA structure, development and governance processes.

But it is not the Enterprise Architect, as too often is the case today, but the EA model and its framework to guide all Enterprise developments. Because otherwise your smart EA architect would become your major bottleneck and risk. Once the EA and the framework achieve a mature state, the EA governance framework, created by the architect, should guide the enterprise change and transformation from then on. The EA architect would still oversee the development but the architect will automate in fact the EA work, adoption, usage... by creating EA checkpoints and controls in all relevant processes which the professionals should employ. The Architect will not need to become ubiquitous as a result.

Ideally an EA architect, like an eminent coach, should make oneself redundant once the mission is accomplished.

Given the state of the EA frameworks today, the Enterprise Architect, the one who models the enterprise, must often build own framework. Therefore the architect must have a structured mind and a disposition or call for structuring systems and experience thereof.

The Chief EA architect responsibilities and EA team job description is to:

- put together the EA business case to justify the EA development once for all so that nobody asks again and again **"***after all, why are we doing this***"?)**
- sell EA value to the business and management to get sponsorship and resources
- do the EA framework selection and customization and/or design the framework creatively given the current status. This is a critical success factor for the rest of the EA development

because without a proper framework most EA efforts end nowhere. Furthermore the current EA frameworks don't help.

- establish the EA architecture principles that enable the design of the target enterprise
- establish the technology standards, guidelines and roadmaps to simplify incoming technology selections
- set in place the EA development process and its milestones
- break down the EA work into workstreams with coherent deliverables
- organize the teams to discover and document the current Enterprise state, document its blueprint
- map the Business and IT Strategies to EA to project the target EA
- produce the 100 days plan and the long term roadmap
- lead the effort to organize early the EA materials into an taxonomy exposed on the Intranet for stakeholders' understanding, training and usage
- recruit and coach the EA team
- coordinate the entire EA development work
- select the set of IT tools beginning with the EA tool
- periodically prove and communicate that EA returns value by quantifying the benefits to stakeholders who use it
- create the maturity framework, so that the management and interested stakeholders can measure objectively the EA progress and its level of utilisation
- specify the EA compliance criteria and process controls for all business developments
- The EA compliance frame dictates the mechanisms the solution architecture designs need to comply to such as EA principles, components reuse, naming, notations, constraints... EA checkpoints. As such the EA architect would not have to be involved in all enterprise activities, i.e. be the EA factotum but its brains.
- keep up to date the Management, Business, IT and in general all stakeholders so that the EA can be adopted, continuously improved with feedback and increasingly used.

To be able to cover the entire Business operation the EA architect should be positioned at the highest level in the organisation hierarchy.

But most Enterprise Architects today don't do the above

EA architects today do everything in IT but EA. That is, in reality they should not be called EA architects but the Enterprise (IT) Authority or so. They usually validate most business-IT developments against their own professional experience which is good but leads to variable and debatable outcomes because every EA may come with a different outcome.

Yet, in practice the architect must fulfil the role you really need to

.1. deliver the Enterprise Model rather than to TOGAF and Zachman specs

Or

.2. play the role of Enterprise IT Authority that is participate in Decision Boards, oversee solution development processes and deliveries without effectively delivering the EA, as today.

Hence the key role of the EA Architect is to model the enterprise and lead its future Design as opposed to the current EA role of supervising the IT enterprise wide activities.

MODELLING THE ENTERPRISE OF THE FUTURE WITH BUSINESS CAPABILITIES

Modelling with capabilities

There are too many definitions for business capability to even try to expose or reconcile the views on the matter. Suffice to say though that they all ultimately refer to what an enterprise can do, that is an ability to do something, as the dictionary term denotes.

Any system, as a black box, is characterised by a set of capabilities which deliver external services. For example, a TV is capable of receiving signals, decode them, display the resulting image, render the afferent sound or even connect to the Internet.

The term Capability appears to come from the Enterprise Architecture discipline rather than from the business academy or quality assurance and process management (BPM) fields. While often invoked by enterprise architects, it raises questions in the BPM world because it overlaps over the notions of process and process maps. The fact that BPM and EA don't intersect much today may explain why the term appeared in EA in the first place and why it overlaps with the BPM terminology. But further discussion on definitions may lead nowhere, experience says.

But an Enterprise consists of and can be described in terms of its capabilities. The enterprise can even be logically partitioned in its key capabilities.

Enterprises can be compared by looking at their sets of capabilities.

Capabilities are identified in the first place by the enterprise Use Cases. There are too the internal capabilities that deliver internally into the Value Chain and offer support to the other capabilities.

Since, in practice, a capability is implemented in a more or less effective manner, it may be quantified in terms of capacity, quality and components or features. Capabilities can be compared as such.

A capability can be also seen as a component of another capability. Capabilities are hence hierarchical, that is, made of other capabilities.

Most companies develop competency in a few "core" capabilities that differentiate them from competition. Most other capabilities could be then outsourced to expert providers.

Stakeholders though "see" different sets of capabilities.

The users of a telco services are concerned with such capabilities as voice, data, streaming, games, music download... services. Partners and suppliers may be interested, for instance, in the order processing, invoicing and Business to Business (B2B) capabilities. To a corporate, the capability of interest would be the Virtual Private Network offer. To a maps service provider, the location services capability. To an investor, the capabilities would be structured in terms of profit returns. An enterprise modeller must assess and describe the capabilities from all these stakeholders' viewpoints.

Capabilities are a useful concept for the business, in particular in the context of strategy implementation, since they have the potential to map the business goals to the technical and human resources affiliated. Because, under the hood, capabilities rely on the resources that make them possible. A process alone is an abstract concept, that is, it cannot deliver without the resources that implement it. The Capability notion as such includes the executing resources such as people and technology.

Since capabilities consists of functional elements and the physical resources that implement them, they bridge the worlds of business and technology. While the business would map their requirements and strategy to capabilities, the architects would further cascade them to technology and organisation. Thus, capabilities are useful in enterprise analysis and strategy execution.

Capabilities though overlap in terms of business Functions, process and implementation resources. While there is no standardised set of capabilities for an enterprise, they are typically illustrated in bespoke capability maps. But, like the "breathing" ability of a human body, a capability is the result of a complex process, involving many functions, rather than a single structural element. Still, high level capabilities can be identified with whole Functions of the Enterprise.

A capability map is a list of capabilities often illustrated as boxes on a sheet of paper representing the enterprise. In Enterprise Architecture, a capability map is too often seen as a functions map, that is a grouping of similar processes, sometimes aligned to a value chain. But capabilities are, typically, neither pure processes nor functions. In any case, it is seldom that a single Function implements a capability. The Function must contain the Flow that delivers the capability outcome. But, at a high level, Functions and Capabilities look similar though and are somewhat interchangeable, because a Function may consist of an internal Flow. Moreover, Functions, Flows Capabilities, they all consist of elementary processes.

Currently though, in the Enterprise Architecture field, a capability is too often narrowly interpreted as an isolated node (see capability maps), often part of a flow. that is, it is seen as a structural element, rather than a general service that is delivered by a flow over nodes and the executing resources. Confounding a major ability of an enterprise with a node may lead to architectural miss-approaches. It is not the capability concept that is wrong but its interpretation that is over simplified as a node. For example, a capability map is interpreted as the structure/architecture of the enterprise while it is mainly a list.

A car has the capability to illuminate the road ahead. But this capability is not implemented in a single element, the light bulb. It is the outcome of the operation of a battery, generator, wiring, switches, fuses, light bulbs... all described by the "lighting ahead" capability architecture.

A capability map is neither a business nor an enterprise architecture. Even if, at first sight, a map does look like an architecture, it is not so since the capability boxes in the map are not interconnected and are not nodes in an architecture but, usually, composites of nodes, links, information and flows.

A capability must be represented as an architecture view, illustrated in terms of the other architecture elements. But because a capability is not represented today in such terms, capabilities overlap and even compete in concept with processes, functions and flows. And, unfortunately a capability map is too often equalled to a business architecture, which indeed, is a gross simplification.

But once we can properly represent a capability in terms of EA components we can map business strategy to architecture, compare and build capabilities. And we can finally, embrace them.

In this work, the capability is defined in terms of EA elements such as function, process, services, value streams, systems, applications...

In summary, a capability describes as such the section of a system that deliveries it in a set of diagrams illustrating the functions, links, flows and the implementation resources that implement the capability. A capability is implemented in at least a structural node of a system. But associating a capability with a single node is the most current misinterpretation that mars the usage of capability.

A capability map is rarely though, if at all, used by the business today even though capabilities can be employed to cascade the business intent to resources.

Because a capability is typically more than a process, a capability map should not quite equal a process map even if they look alike. Hence, the existing process maps, such as APQC, eTOM..., are not really employed as capability maps. In fact, Standards Organisations produce their own capability industry reference maps today which unfortunately look very much like the Business Process Maps which we already have. We need not duplicate these previous efforts though.

In short, a capability

- is what a system/an enterprise can do
- delivers an outcome to an enterprise stakeholder
- consists of business processes and the resources, people and technology, that enable it
- can be decomposed hierarchically
- consist, of a Flow, a sequence of processes executed in function(s) since they deliver an outcome,
- implement system/enterprise Use Cases since they deliver outcomes/value to each external stakeholder
- implement internal services, in the most general sense

The Future of Enterprise Design, Business Capabilities as a Service, BCaaS

Architects often specify today capability maps. A Capability is something an enterprise can do. As such a capability map defines illustrates what the entire enterprise can do.

The capability concept though is too vague to be of service in any practical application. It has no scope, delimiting perimeter, workflows, components, interfaces, services, outcomes, implementation... As such a capability today is hard to delimit and realise in practice. We cannot use the capability map to roadmap, construct or depict an enterprise because, except for their boxy appearance, the map still constitutes a simple list of business key words of little significance for any enterprise stakeholder.

Bust since the concept of capability has value, it makes sense to refine it so that it can be used in the enterprise characterisation, planning, strategy or even construction. Moreover, since most capabilities are common to most enterprises, it makes sense to outsource them to expert service providers because they can build, manage, scale, secure, maintain and update them better, cheaper and faster than any enterprise. Nevertheless, to be outsourceable, capabilities must be autonomous and deliver their common services over rather standard interfaces so that they can be reused.

The Business Capability as a Service, BCaaS

Proposed here is the concept of Business Capability as a Service (BCaaS). The BCaaS would solve the problems of the poor definition and delimitation of capabilities, rendering them implementable and outsourceable as such.

A BCaaS is an autonomous capability, consisting of a group of related business functions and workflows plus the technology and people that execute them, that delivers its services over an interface. The implementation is encapsulated and as such hidden from clients. Hence, the clients do not have to be aware or deal with the organisation and the technology of implementation. A BCaaS, in addition to a capability, is realisable because it is well defined, implementable, with its services exposed through interfaces.

In fact, the BCaaS refines the capability concept the same way a SOA service refines the notion of "service" today. The terms BCaaS and SOA Service denote in practice the same concept in this view. Yet, capabilities are at the Enterprise level of granularity, that is a much larger granularity. The BCaaS looks in principle like a Cloud service which is delivered though by people, not only technology. For people actions though reaction time is reasonable longer. But BCaaSs may contain smaller capabilities and services. A BCaaS must be specified at the Enterprise Architecture level though. In fact, the enterprise architecture can be expressed now as a BCaaS Map which can be employed to construct and plan the enterprise.

To be fair, the concept is not new, see Capability as a Service by CaaS, an European project: "CaaS – Capability as a Service for Digital Enterprises. FP 7 ICT Programme Collaborative Project no: 611351: Capabilities refer to essential functions of the enterprise that link business goals to business processes, resources and actors. These capabilities are mapped onto IT solutions, such as software services, that are delivered to customers... To this end, the CaaS project will deliver the Capability Driven Development (CDD) approach".

Yet, the outcome of this work, a Capability Driven Development made little further progress so far but in the academic milieu. Then, the people component seemed to have been left aside, with CaaS implemented in IT alone. And, since the CaaS concept was not introduced in the Enterprise Architecture context, it has the same fate as enterprise SOA since nobody identified first the SOA services at the enterprise level.

The BCaaS concept proposed here though emphasises a capability as an enterprise block. Starting from a top level Business Architecture, identified here are the key capabilities of a generic industry enterprise. With these Business Capabilities as a Service we may then describe, roadmap and build an Enterprise.

The way forward seems to be an enterprise constructed of off-the-shelf standard capabilities, just like a Lego. In the future, an enterprise could be quickly built of autonomous capability blocks provided eventually by 3rd parties, i.e. Business Capabilities as a Service, BCaaSs. Only the core services that offer a competitive advantage might still be operated by the enterprise. There will be little or no IT in the enterprise. The costly IT procurement, licensing, maintenance, upgrades would become now a thing of the past. The IT will be part of each Business Capability i.e. not an enterprise concern. All common capabilities that bring no value to the Business Model can be also outsourced.

But this future will happen gradually, beginning small because the market has yet to provide such BCaaS capabilities. What suppliers miss today is the top down enterprise picture where everyone can pinpoint the capabilities that form an enterprise. Enterprise SOA died in the absence of the SOA enterprise level services.

The paper here aims to provide this complete enterprise business capability framework. Further on, it is further shown how an enterprise can be assembled out of less than 20 BCaaSs and how an Enterprise Capability as a Service, ECaaS capability could be employed even more simply to build and tailor a new enterprise. Hence, once the BCaaSs functionality is defined by this framework, the capabilities could be constructed by key suppliers.

In conclusion, the BCaaS concept is a blend of the Capability and SOA services concepts defined at the top enterprise level.

GODS single page Business Architecture

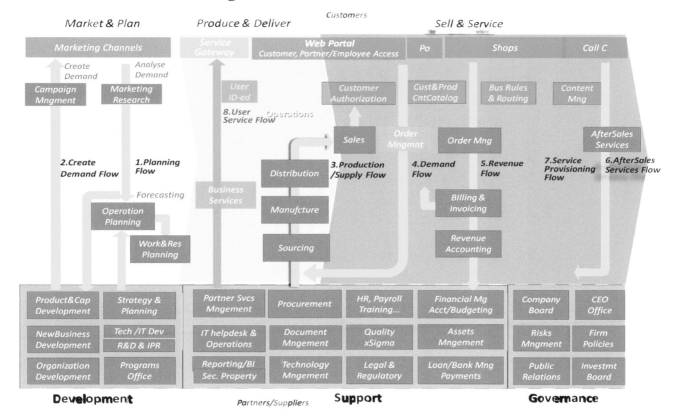

The Gas To Liquids One Page Business Architecture, an application of GODS

And here is an application of the GODS one page Business Architecture for an enterprise in the Gas to Liquids Industry. The GTL Architecture is organised in the Enterprise GODS (Governance – Operations – Development and Support) structure.

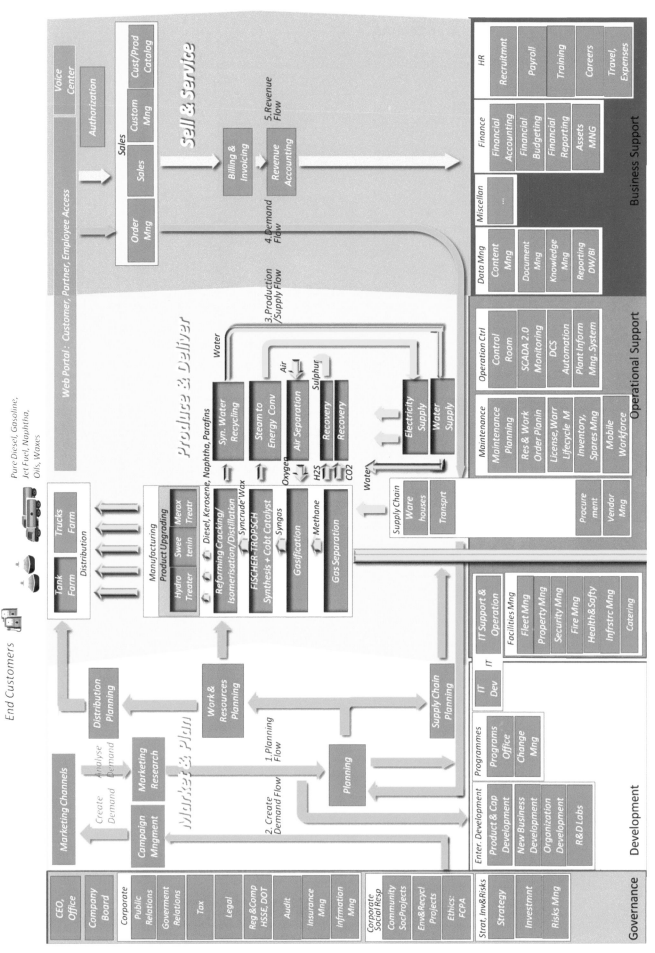

Capabilities assessed on Business Architecture

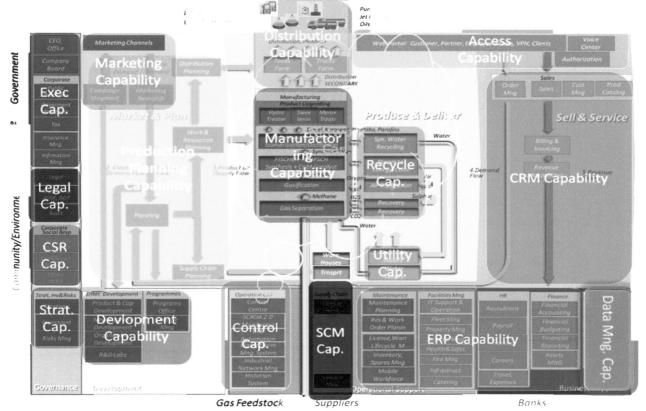

The Enterprise Capability Map

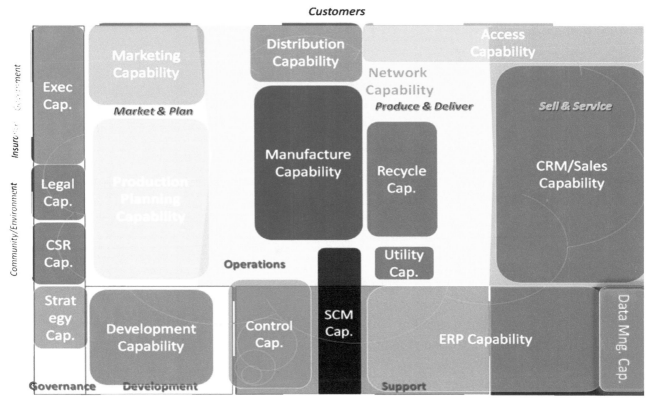

Governance capabilities

1. Executive Management Capability
   a. Company Board Function
   b. CEO Office Function
   c. Public Relations Management Function
   d. Government Relations Management Function
   e. Tax Management Function
   f. Insurance Management Function
   g. Information Management Function
2. Legal Management Capability
   a. Legal Management Function
   b. Regulatory & Compliance Management Function
   c. Audit Management Function
3. Corporate Social Responsibility Management Capability
   a. Community relations and Social Projects Management
   b. Environment & Recycling
   c. Ethics, FCPA (Foreign Corrupt Practices Act) Management
4. Strategy, Investment and Risks Management Capability
   a. Strategy Function Management
   b. Investment Function Management
   c. Risks Management Function

Operations Capabilities

Market & Plan

5. Marketing Management
   a. Marketing Channels
   b. Campaign Management
   c. Marketing Research
6. Enterprise Forecasting and Planning
   a. Distribution Planning
   b. Operations and Planning
   c. Supply Chain Planning

Produce & Deliver

7. Distribution
8. Production/Manufacturing
9. Recovery & Recycling automation
10. Utilities Delivery/Management

Sales & Service

11. Access Capability
    a. Web Portal Access Capability
    b. Voice Centre Access Capability
    c. Authorisation Access Capability
    d. Remote Access Capability
12. Customer Relationship Management
    a. Order Management
    b. Customer Management

c. Sales Management
d. Product Catalogue and Information
e. Billing and Invoicing
f. Revenue Accounting

Development Capabilities

13. Enterprise Development Capability
    a. Product and Capability Management Capability
    b. New Business Development Management Capability
    c. Organisation Development Management Capability
    d. R&D Management Capability
    Programmes Management
    e. Programmes Office Capability
    f. Change Management Capability

Support Capabilities

14. Supply Chain Management Operation
    a. Sourcing
    b. Transport/Warehousing for parts
    c. Procurement
    d. Vendor Management
15. Enterprise Resource Planning Capability
    a. Maintenance Capability
        i. Maintenance Planning Service
        ii. Resources and Workers Planning Service
        iii. Licences, Warranties and Lifecycle Service
        iv. Inventory and Spares Management Service
        v. Mobile Workforce Planning Service
    b. Facilities Management Capability
        i. IT Support and Operation Service
        ii. Security Management Service
        iii. Fleet and Parking Management Service
        iv. Property Management Service
        v. Health and Safety Management Service
        vi. Fire Management Service
        vii. Catering Management Service
        viii. Infrastructure Management Service
    c. Human Resources
        i. Recruitment Service
        ii. Payroll Service
        iii. Training Service
        iv. Careers and Problem Resolution Service
        v. Travel and Expenses Service
    d. Finance
        i. Financial Accounting Service
        ii. Budgeting Service
        iii. Financial Reporting Service
        iv. Assets Management Service
16. Data Management

    a. Content Management
    b. Document Management
    c. Knowledge Management
    d. Reporting DW/BI
17. Operations Control Capability
    a. Control Centre
    b. Monitoring (SCADA2.0)
    c. DCS Automation
    d. Plant Information Management System
    e. Operations Network Management
    f. Historian System

The Broker Function

A Broker company may provide to an enterprise, integrate and manage all the enterprise common functions outsourced from various suppliers:

Broker responsabilities:

- ○ procurement of capabilities
- ○ Integration glue that ties the capabilities together in flows and links them to the enterprise
- ○ maintenance, fixing, updating and upgrading of capabilities
- ○ provides a single unified source of data
- ○ single source of charging and billing

The Enterprise and the constituent Capabilities

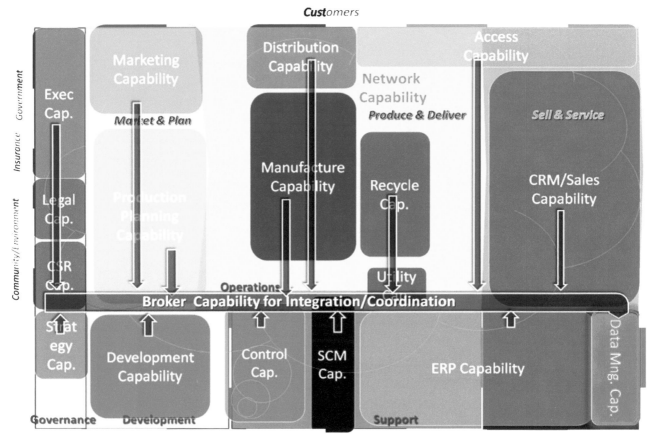

How to build your enterprise with Capabilitiues

.A. Customise the big picture one page GODS Business Architecture for your enterprise.

.B. Tailor the generic GODS capabilities map to your enterprise

.C. Research the market for suppliers of capabilities and integration services. Iterate.
Look for

- Cloud services for which you may provide the qualified personnel to operate
- BPO Services (Business Process Outsourcing) – a BPO service includes the manpower
- or decide to provide the capability internally

.D. Chose a broker which selects, provides and integrates your capabilities

from 3rd parties. The enterprise willwork with the broker rather than each supplier in part.

The Enterprise as a Service Capability

Down the line, we may think of an Enterprise Capability as a Service (ECaaS) as the highest possible level of capability that can be provided off-the-shelf for an enterprise. It should offer most enterprise support functionality off-the shelf tailored eventually for various industries. Any enterprise may be built with an ECaaS and the competitive advantageous own BCaaSs.

Why would you build your own HR, Finance, Strategy, Manufacturing, Sales... from scratch when you can benefit from such full capabilities provided as integrated Business Capabilities as a Service by firms which do this on a large scale, firms which have the best of breed applications and already trained people? If the features, QoS and cost are right then you have to just pay on demand according to your plan.

The Enterprise as a Service Capability

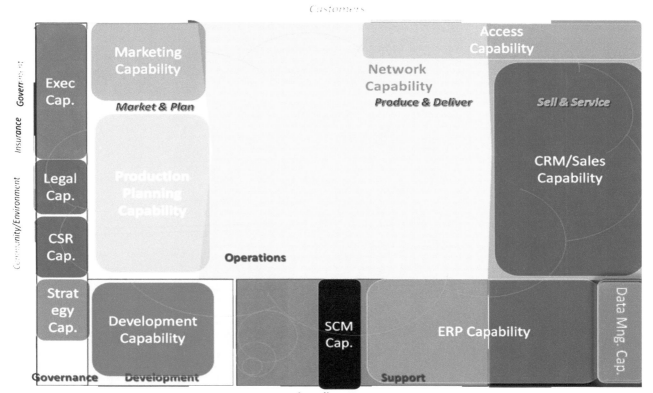

What an enterprise has to achieve today is results, i.e. best quality products, profit to investors and value to employees and, in general, to all stakeholders, including the community and the environment, rather than bother with support services such as recruiting, training, team building, buying and maintaining applications... This will be left to the Firm providing the Enterprise Capability as a Service, ECaaS capability. It is their business. Yours is to produce and sell more of your products.

Moreover, a must characteristic of an enterprise today is Agility. That can be achieved on a competitive level only by constructing the enterprise with interchangeable blocks (BCaaS) that can be swapped as needed to perform and deliver.

Summary

The Business Capability as a Service, BCaaS, concept proposed in this article refines the existing capability paradigm at the enterprise level so that capabilities can be properly delimited and autonomously implemented and delivered. BCaaSs are as such effectively enterprise level services which implementation and delivery can be outsourced.

The BCaaS capabilities are illustrated then as the building blocks of a top level generic GODS Enterprise Architecture Capability framework. Hence, to build and plan an enterprise, one can employ between the 20 to 50 enterprise BCaaSs built on premise by or outsourced to capability suppliers or a Broker which will supply the a number of integrated capabilities to the enterprise and a single source of data and integration to the enterprise.

Hence this approach proposes a large granularity *Enterprise as a Service* capability, supplied by a Broker, which   supplies most common enterprise capabilities and services integrated as one so that the enterprise itself would only have to come with its business model and competitive capabilities.

Thus the ECaaS capability looks very much like the Enterprise ERP for an industry. IT would consist of

- Governance functions such as Corporate Social Responsibility, Legal...
- Operational capabilities such as Marketing, Plan, Source, Make, Deliver, Sales and Services
- Development capabilities such as Strategy and Business and New Product Development...
- Support activities such as ERP- Finance, HR..., IT support

In the end, the enterprise can only provide the Governance Decision Making capability. Even the enterprise coordination function can be outsourced to the Broker.

STRATEGY DESIGN AND MAPPING, THE STRATEGY POSTER

The analysis and strategy specification process is typically executed by the business strategy team as an Enterprise wide collaborative effort. Nevertheless, as it significantly impacts the target model the strategy specification process is outlined here.

 Outline the vision, goals of the company and in quantifiable terms, the targets. This is an iterative process since goals must be tested against reality. A vision must take into account strengths & opportunities, competencies and assets but is as well, an ambition

S-1 Employ this strategy development process

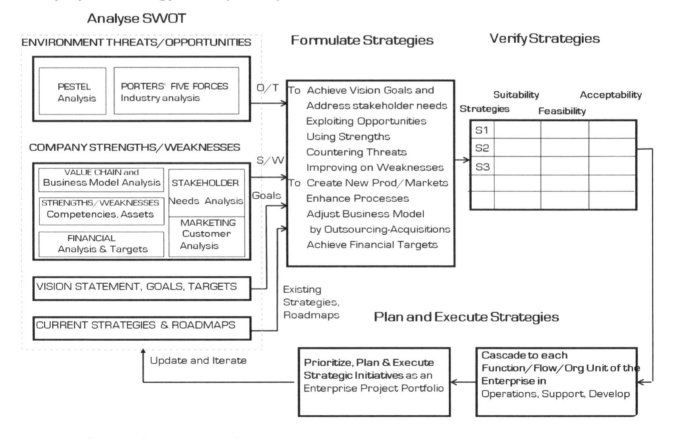

S-2 Employ/Tailor the Strategy Rings Framework

The Trends in the macro environment, the markets, competitors and, in general, Porter's Five forces, the strengths and weaknesses of the current enterprise and the existing strategy and enterprise vision, all concur in shaping the strategies that then map onto the business capabilities of the enterprise.

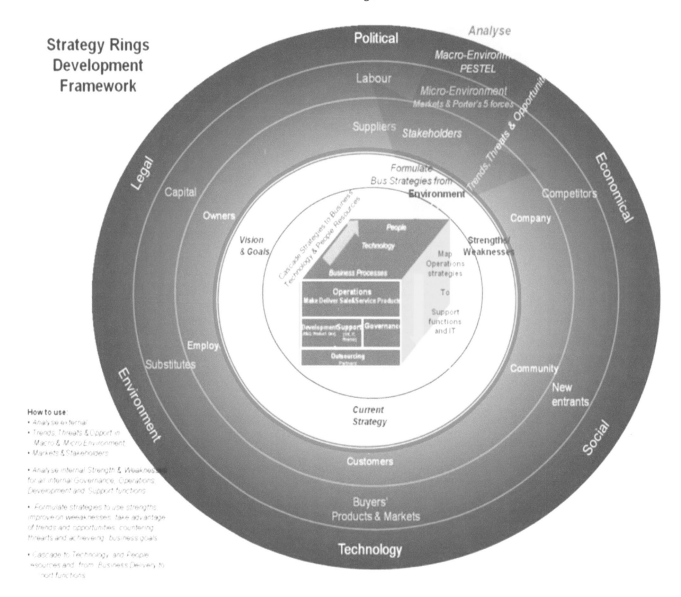

S-3 Do Environment Analysis: PESTEL, Porter's 5 Forces

Strategy and Enterprise Architecture are about long term thinking.

Strategy has to take into account, long term, the Economical, Political, Social, Environmental and Regulatory forces in the macro-environment. The analysis process will reveal Trends, Opportunities and Threats (O/T) which, once known and acted upon, would permit the company to adapt to this increasingly competitive world.

Identify your specific industry environment, your competitors, substitutes, suppliers and customers' trends and discover your company's core competencies and weaknesses… Do PESTEL (Political, Economical, Social, Technology, Environment, Legal) and Porter's Five Forces (Customers, Suppliers, Competitors, New Entrants, Substitutes) analysis, both often used by business to study the macro-environment. A PESTEL, Porter's Five Forces analysis and the resulting trends and recommendations are given in the following:

PESTEL

Political and Regulatory/Legal

- increasing taxation trend
- new EU laws

- new economical super-blocks: China…
- growing likelihood of terrorist attacks
- privacy laws strengthening
- new financial compliance regulation

Economical

- expansion in new markets (China, East Europe…, Africa)
- reducing time to market
- industry consolidation
- increasing energy prices
- changes in own Value Chain for outsourcing and M&A

Social/Cultural/Demographics

- increase concern for Corporate Social Responsibility
- aging population
- growing need for remote work
- globalization
- travel to remote world spots

Technology Trends

- new customer satisfaction levels, in terms of service quality, service discovery, usability, response time, availability and customer care
- growing amount of info (Data Architecture, Data Warehousing, Business Intelligence, Content Management …)
- growing concern for data privacy, integrity and confidentiality
- increasing technology capabilities (processing power, storage, network bandwidth…)
- mounting complexity
- accelerating rate of technological change (scenario modelling, decision making, portfolio management)
- trend for virtualization technologies for Storage, Network & Processing (On Demand/Utility Computing, Grid Computing, OS virtualization, Blades…)
- growing requirement for converged networks and terminals (Internet, telecoms, IP networks, broadcast…)
- need for continuous availability of business and disaster recovery

Environmental

- growing concern for Corporate and Social Responsibility (CSR) (waste, packaging, radiation, recycling, re-use…)

Porter's Five Forces

Customers

- Prepare for increasing proportion of aged customers
- Devise web buying and distribution channels

Suppliers

- Affected by super mergers and acquisitions
- Prices going up with green policies and petrol costs

Competitors

- Prepare strategy against new low entry competitors

- Design strategy to compete with high end operators

Substitutes

- Establish strategy to mitigate substitutes, reducing your market share

S-4 Do Stakeholders' analysis

The enterprise strategy needs to deliver value to each and every stakeholder beginning with the Customer, Owner, Employee and Company. People (employees) are an important stakeholder and company asset, capable of returning value for years, if properly invested in, or holding down your company because of a culture of politics. For Each stakeholder, analyze ways to enhance returns.

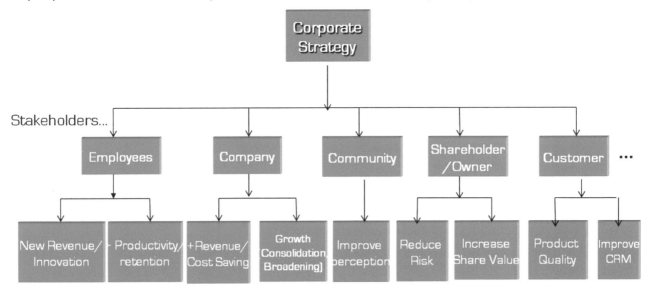

S-5 Do Company Analysis

Analyse the Value Chains and business models of the company, its financial performance and targets, its organization and evolution, business processes and current strategies and objectives.

Do a high level Business Process and Value Chain analysis. Do you need to automate processes or improve the performance of key processes? Is there an opportunity to specialize on a link in the value chain or else outsource it? Is there a skills shortage (weakness)? What are the strengths of the firm? Financial analysis will reveal how effectively business is conducted and will enable you to establish new targets to stimulate investment. Marketing research will provide answers with regard to new products or markets (segments) the company may need to deliver and approach.

S-6 Specify Strategies

The results of the analysis (PESTEL trends, Opportunities and Threats (O/T), Company Strengths and Weaknesses (S/W), process improvements, new Value Chain and business models ...) enable you to formulate strategies as actions to be performed in the long term.

At this stage you have a vision and targets for the To-Be Enterprise. Re-consider current strategies and morph them into new ones. For instance, develop strategies for:

Customers to

- integrate access channels and provide internet access and self service
- deliver new products and/or new market segments

Owners/Shareholders to

- deliver increased value for their investment (dividends)
- prevent risks and take advantage of opportunities

Company to

- transform the company for agility (flexibility, adaptability, scalability …)
- prepare for growth (mergers & acquisitions)
- prepare for SOA< Cloud and outsourcing
- reduce costs of operation
- enhance brand image

Community/Environment/Regulatory

- protect the environment, enhance community benefits
- comply with regulations

Employee (People) to

- Improve business and technical skills
- transform culture

Here is another view of the Strategy Rings framework illustrating elements in each circle.

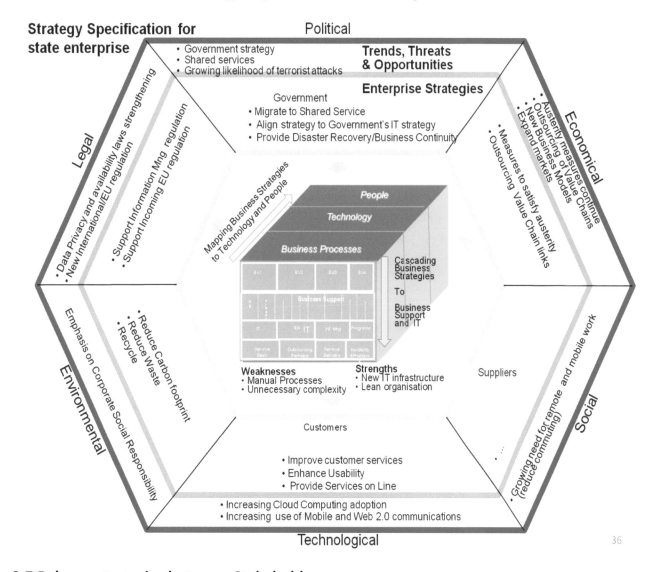

S-7 Balance strategies between Stakeholders

This diagram should help the strategist establish an equilibrium in formulating the strategies. None of the stakeholders should be left out in the consideration of benefits returned by strategies.

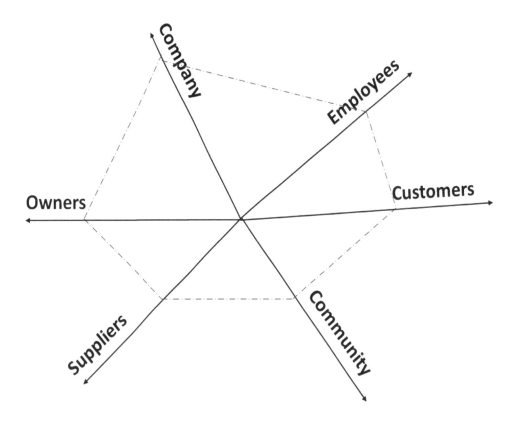

Balance Benefits for each Stakeholder since there are conflicting interests

15. S-8 Check Strategies for Suitability, Feasibility, Acceptability
Suitability: is the strategy delivering the goals? Verify the appropriateness of a strategy, based on company's strategic goals (check against vision and goals).

16. **Feasibility:** can you do it? Asses if the company has the resources and capabilities (core competencies, assets, strengths) to deliver the strategies.

17. **Acceptability:** is the potential cost in the realm of possibility? Is the strategy serving the stakeholders? Decide if the strategy is achievable in terms of financial returns and delivery timescales. Evaluate again the outcomes in the light of stakeholders' expectations (including community, regulatory) and financial results (business cases).

S-9 Sum up strategies in Strategy table

IT Strategy	Business Support Group Strategies	Stakeholder Business Groups	Enterprise Strategies	External Drivers
• Implement DR mechanism	• Implement BC processes	Business Support	• Do DR/BC anti terrorist attacks	*Political*
• Provide FOI, DPA, Records Manag.	• Develop Information Management support	BusinessSupport	• Information Management regulation	*Legal/ Regulatory*
• Reduce Infrastructure footprint • Reduce printing (paper) • Automatic shut-offs PCs /servers	• Create IT program • Reduce # of Data Centres • Refresh technology • Provide recycling support...	Business Support	• Reduce Carbon footprint • Reduce Waste • Recycle	*Environment (CSR)*
• Implement EA and design IT strategy to reduce duplication	• Simplify enterprise operation to reduce costs	Business Support	• Apply austerity targets • Outsourcing Value Chain links	*Economical*
• Outsource (SaaS) non-core functions and licensing activities	• Analyse Value Chain and outsource non core services			
• Provide and Implement solution for Performance Managm./Reporting	• Provide Performance Management reports to Board	Business Support Finance	• Provide performance KPIs to stakeholders	*Government*
• Improved process and design for services to citizens	• Enhance Customer Service Usability	Business Support Transformation	• Improve customer services	*Citizens*
• Develop new services	• Provide new services	Consumer Group	• Provide services to customer needs	*Citizens*
• Study and Improve ERP User Interface and usability	• Increase HR work efficiency	Business Support HR	Reduce taxpayers costs	*Citizens*
• Implement Video Conferencing	• Reduce cost of travel	Business Support Facilities	• Reduce taxpayer costs	*Citizens*

• Rationalise /simplify IT landscape
• Improve SAP user interfaces
• Implement Federated Sign On
• Reduce cost of CRM solution
• Provide employee Single Sign On
• Introduce automation
• Migrate to Open Source and Cloud
• Document ed to end processes
	• Improve internal systems usability
	• Apply Architecture principles to
	  • re-use, consolidation, standardisation, open source
		Business Support Transformation/ICT	• **Remedy Weaknesses like**
			  • Duplications
			  • Manual processes
			  • Undocumented practices
			  • Supplier dependence
			• **Employ strengths**
			  • New technology
			  • Streamlined organization
				Company

ANNEX 1. MODELLING AN AIRLINE, ARTEFACTS, THE DESIGN POSTER

The Design is the generic Enterprise Model consisting of the joined-together individual models which components are interlinked in metamodel relationships. The EMintegrates all existing models, otherwise designed and used independently, in a navigable whole. The Design is a natural outcome of a design that takes into consideration the EM framework, its metamodel and principles. The chapter and poster exhibit sample one page architecture diagrams for an airline. It is worth mentioning the limited extent to which an external consultant can design an enterprise model. The detailed work should be done by a virtual team of experts which own their own architecture domains.

At the Business Architecture layer, we design the following diagrams

- The Context diagram, illustrating stakeholders' interactions Including products
- The enterprise Lines of Business and their interactions
- The Business structure, as business Functions and lines/pipes, permanent comms channels
- The Flow diagrams that shares with the Business structure the process
- Information Map

The Airline Group Context diagram

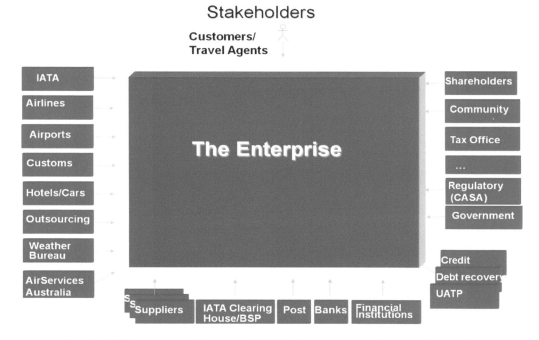

Context Diagram: a diagram of all businesses, systems and people who provide or receive information and services with the system.

The Airline Group Lines of Business (LoBs) and their Value Chains

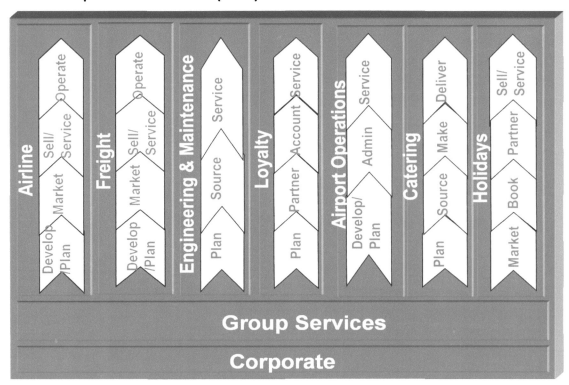

A Business Area or Line of Business (LoB) is an area of the enterprise that delivers a product or service.

The LoB internal interactions diagram for an Airline Group

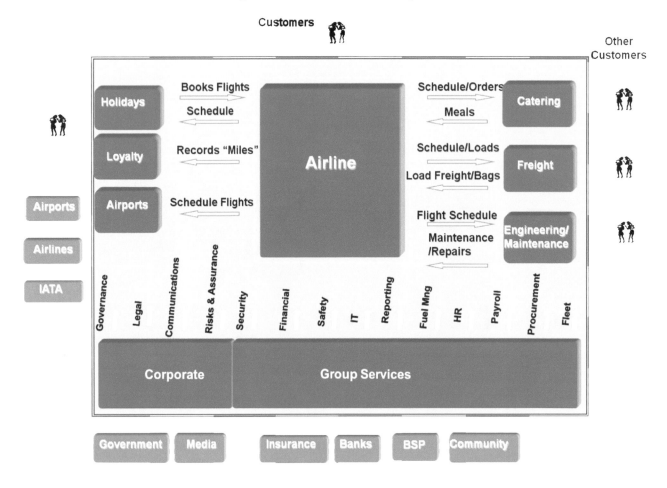

The Business Function Map for an Airline

Determine first the key business activities list from which the Functions can be drafted:

- Researches/Segments market
- Develops products
- Develops airplane fleet
- Schedules multi-leg flights
- Roster crews
- Negotiates Agreements with Airports/Airlines
- Sells/Reserves Seats
- Controls disruptions
- Performs check-in & boarding
- Services passengers
- Transports Bags
- Provides airplane ramp services
- Provides catering and in-flight service

Organise Airline activities organised in GODS structure

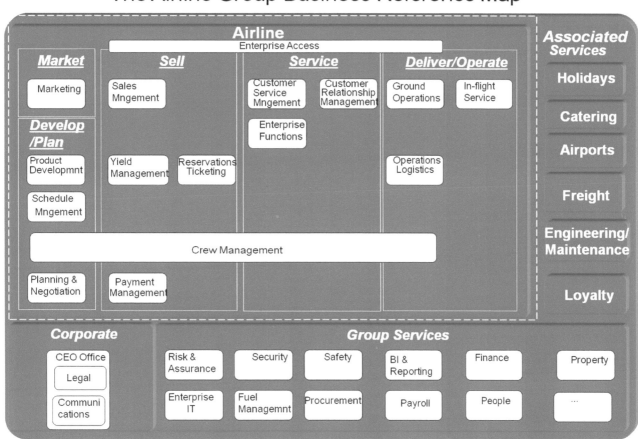

The Airline Group Business Reference Map

The tridimensional Business Functions Map

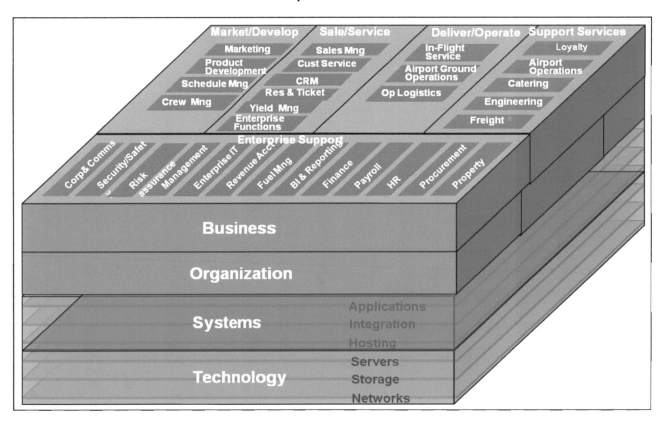

Do Level 2 Airline Business Map

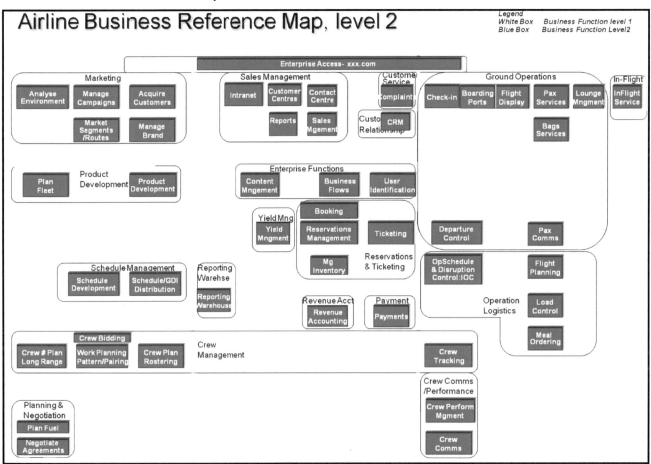

Do the Airline One Page Business Architecture

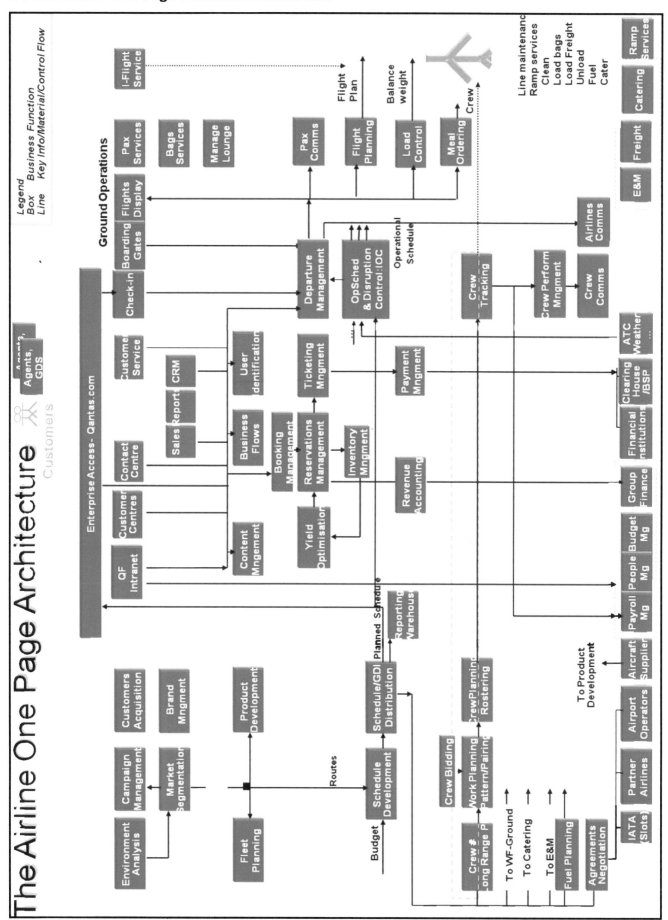

Do the Airline one page Appications Architecture mapped to Business Architecture

In different colours and shades are shown the outsourced applications. A box is a resource i.e. technology system performing a function while in the people diagram a box is the organisation unit.

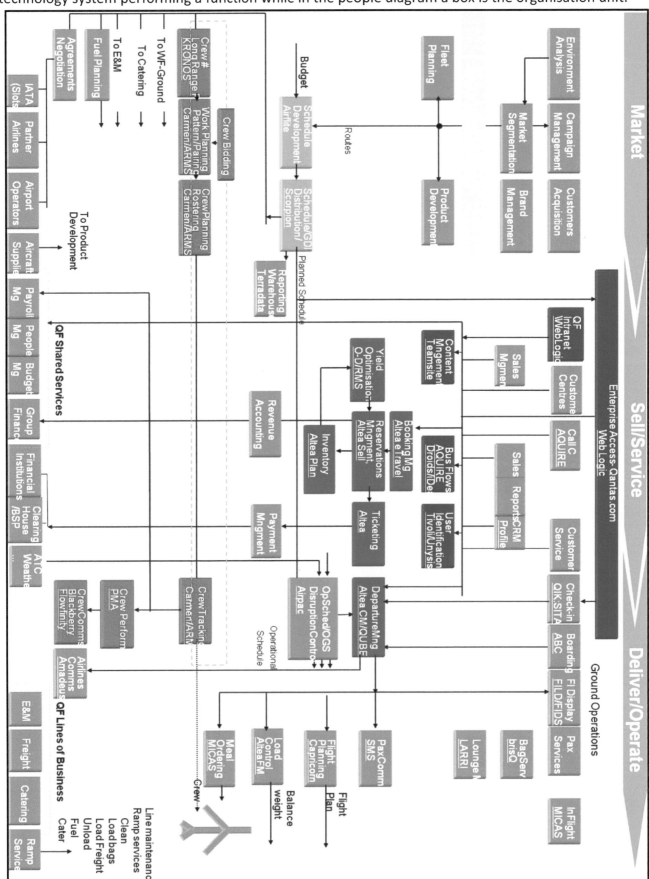

Do Business Flows diagraming sample (non Airline diagram)

Document workflows as in this swimlane to represent the Flows.

https://s-media-cache-ak0.pinimg.com/736x/7a/b6/80/7ab680e4f5bc12a0c33568457bf39976.jpg

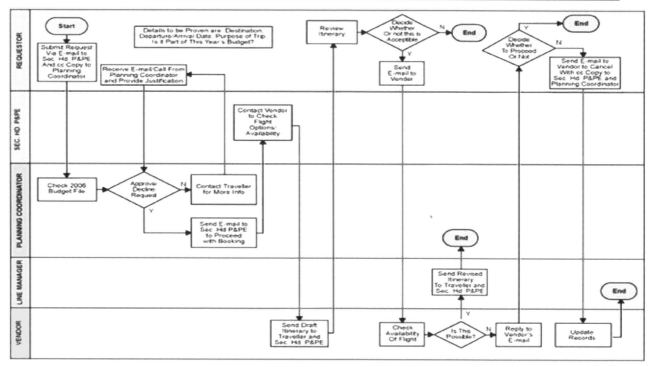

Document Non-IT Technology Architecture (sample)

http://says.com/my/tech/how-satellite-company-inmarsat-tracked-missing-malaysia-airlines-mh370

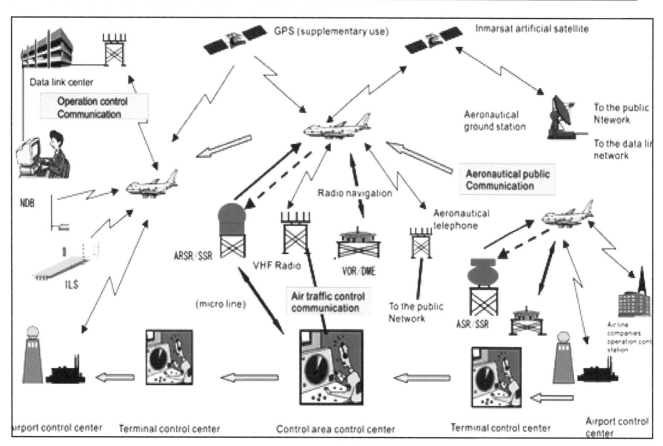

Document Key Information Items

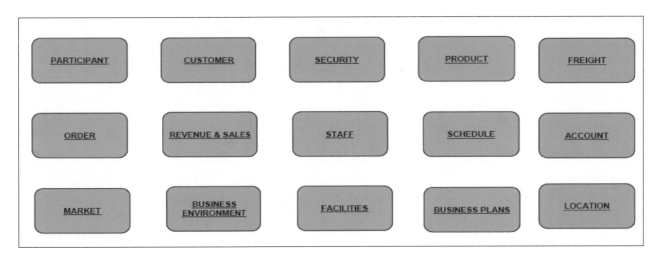

Document Data records/objects in Systems and align to and update Information Items

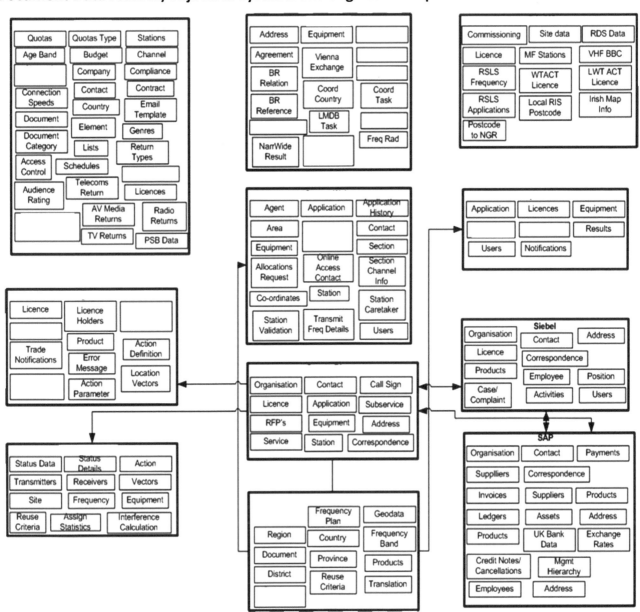

Do Data class/relationships diagrams to illustrate dependencies

Do the data class diagram system independent after you identify the key data records/objects in each system. That will also support the creation of the Master Data.

https://wiki.kuali.org/pages/viewpage.action?pageId=18121767

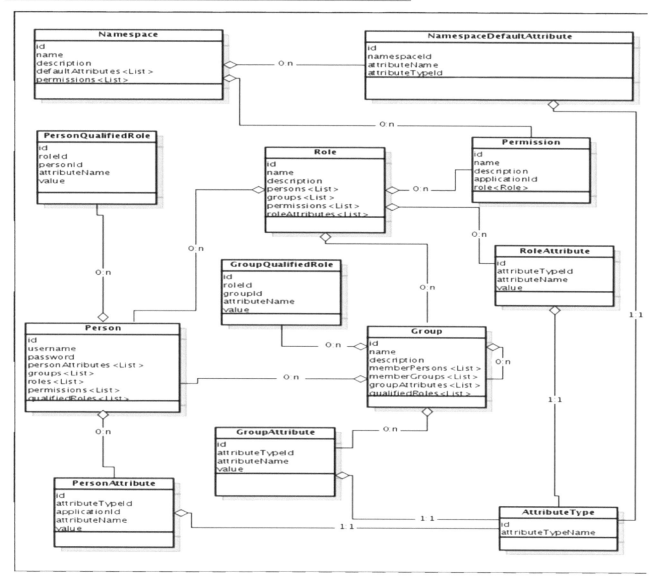

Propose the organisation chart design to align to the Business Functions Map

The Business Functions Map is used here in the design of the Organisation chart. The organization is typically aligned to Business Functions to enable the proper ownership of functionality by the organisational units.

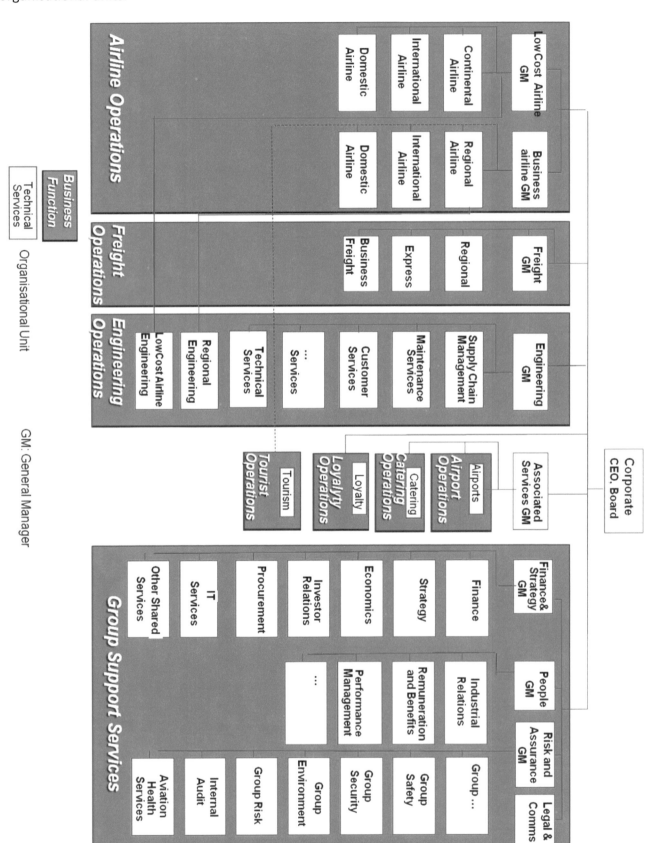

Sketch the first Airline Enterprise Model in 2D as the set of key models linked by metamodel

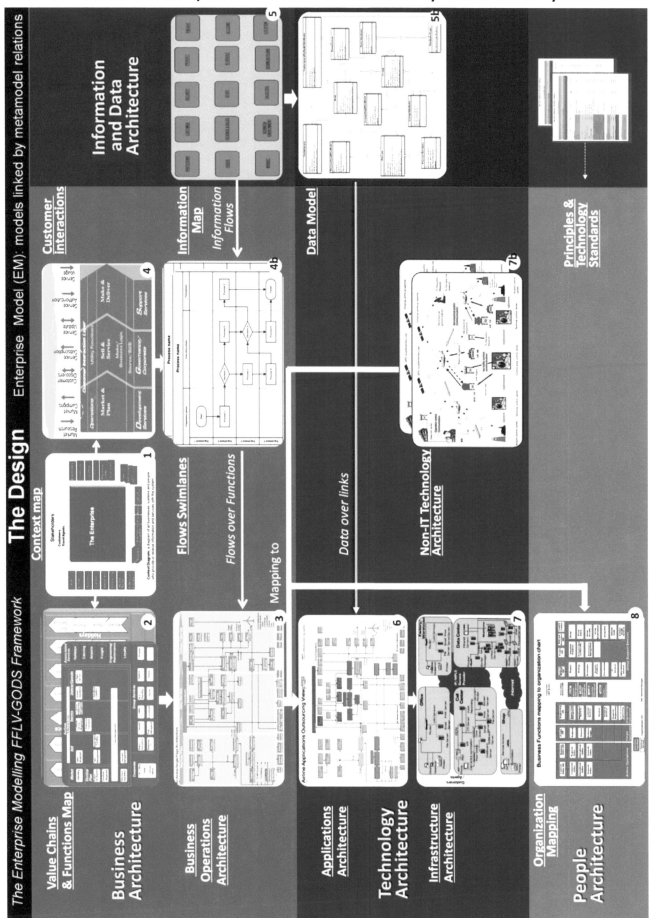

The Airline Enterprise Composite Model in 3D

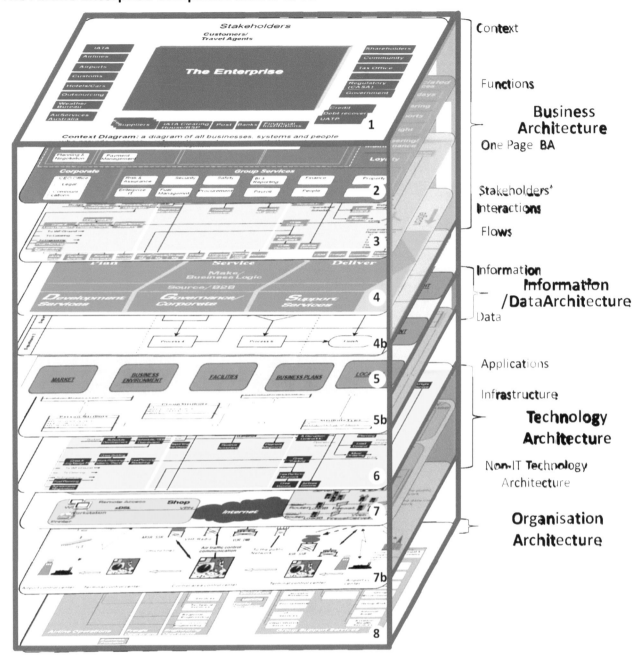

ANNEX 2. MODELLING IT ORGANISATION AND OPERATION, THE ITOOF FRAMEWORK

Most IT service management frameworks, including IT4IT, insert in the IT Cycle/Value Chain the Development Stage rendering the IT cycle

Strategy > (Transition) > Development > Operations > (Improvement).

ITSM frameworks look as such as DevOps but without having any means to support it.

Since the mission of IT Operations is to "Keep the IT lights on" and the aim of Development is to create new capabilities, they should be kept in separate cycles or Value Chains, unless DevOps, which unifies them, is supported at all times.

In addition, the Development and IT Operations cycles are very different, with the Development taking place in a longer frame and in parallel with the IT Operations planning cycle.

Also, while Development demands rapid change, Operations imposes controlled slow change to ensure operations continuity.

The proposed framework here, ITOOF (IT Organisation and Operation Framework) deals with this while reusing the processes of ITIL and reorganising the IT top categories on EA GODS generic architecture.

Use GODS for IT

Applying Enterprise Architecture GODS generic business to IT organisation, the IT Functions are:

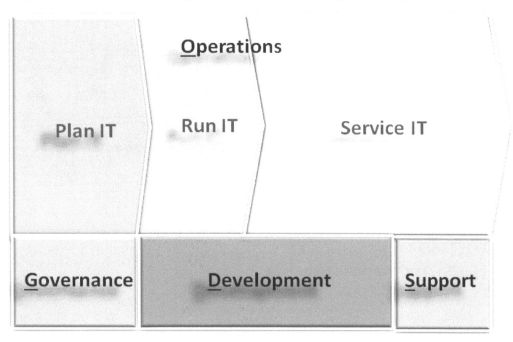

G - IT Governance

O - IT Operations

- o Plan IT
- o Run IT
- o Service IT

D - IT Development

S - IT Support

Add the typical IT Operations to each GODS function

IT Organisation and Operations Architecture Framework

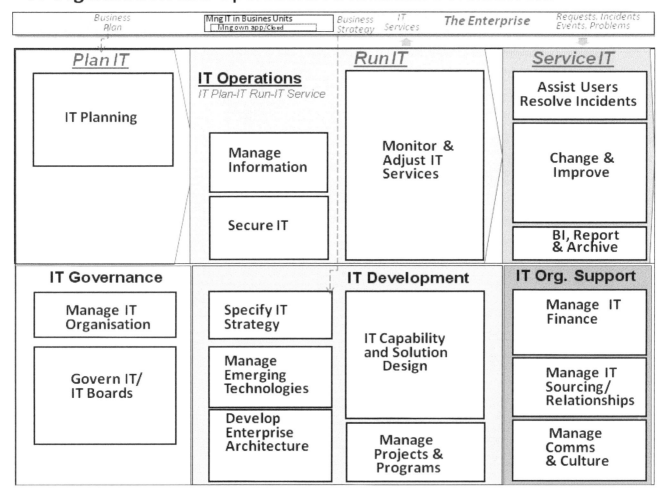

Add the overall IT Flows and existing ITIL Processes to each Function

Add the (cross-)IT Flows

IT Planning Flow

DevOps Flow

Change to Improve Flow

Enterprise Digital Transformation Flow

ITOOF, IT Organisation & Operations Architecture, Capabilities and Flow

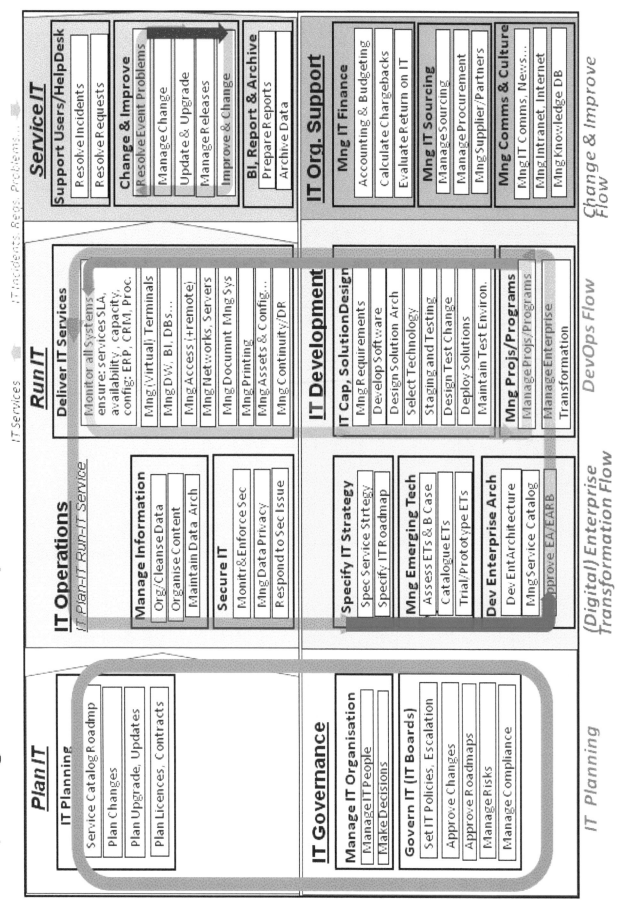

The resulting ITOOF based IT Organization Chart

The IT Functional Organisation Chart

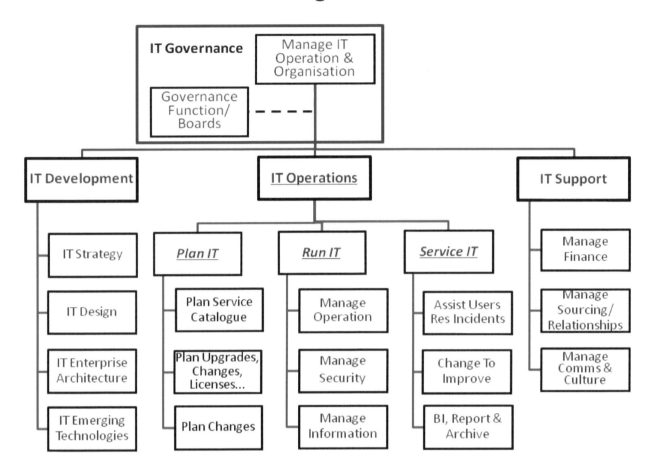

ANNEX 3. OTHER ENTERPRISE MODELLING USE CASES

The EM should be available and used across the company in various ways, to understand, learn, make decisions, for strategic planning, investments and in the design of new products and capabilities.

Framework for Mergers and Acquisitions

The starting point is the existence of two different As-Is Enterprise Architectures, even if not properly documented. The aim is the development and evolution towards a single Enterprise and EA. This is a long term process, finished after the formal merger. To control this process a formal common program has to be established, before the merger, with activities described in this section.

By looking at the EA framework it becomes apparent that you have to align:

.A. the Business layers of the two Enterprises:

Establish the new common Governance of the merged Enterprise

- o   evolve towards a single mission, set of products, market segments,, brands
- o   design a single vision, strategy, objectives

Establish high level logical architecture (business functions and flows); specify common Functions such as operations, shared support and development services; analyze outsourcing at this stage

- o   rationalize external stakeholders (banks, suppliers ...)

.B. the Technology layer

After discovering the existing two EAs, rationalize and standardize the Applications and Infrastructure platforms to serve the functional architecture (Functions and Flows). Decide on, merge and rationalize:

- o   ERP, CRM, SCM...
- o   customer services and sales channels
- o   main product applications
- o   Data Warehouse, Business Intelligence, reporting
- o   B2B platforms
- o   Knowledge and Content management
- o   Voice and IP networks, email and printing architectures
- o   Office technology (PCs, mobiles, Helpdesk, IT support)

.C. Non IT technology and facilities: rationalize real estate, parking...

.D. the People layer:

- o   align organizations to the same EA business functions;

- o manage change (expectations, redundancies...)
- o begin cultural transformation: choose common values, ethics...
- o design common communications channels and technology
- o align payroll levels, recruitment standards...
- o design common EA Views, such as
- o Financial/Accounting functions, flows people and technology
- o data architecture (vocabulary)
- o common security
- o common planning

Framework for Outsourcing

Outsourcing, a fast growing trend, offers the flexibility to choose the best of breed service and cost effective supplier. It could be justified by a few factors:

- reduced costs of service compared to the in house TCO
- enhanced reliability and quality of service as a result of clients' usage by and feedback
- improved response times and productivity through supplier's specialist expertise
- faster time to market due to the new service deployment time
- elimination of longer internal feature development cycles
- minimization of the HW/SW infrastructure maintenance costs
- reduction in real estate for people and machinery.

Moreover, it allows you to focus on managing the key business functions only and deploy an "on demand" model of usage rather than build, operate and maintain, in-house, a service you seldom consume (recruitment for instance).

Drawbacks: the formal, contractual way to address a new requirement, especially when you missed the opportunity to formulate the feature at acquisition. Not all functions can be easily outsourced. The more connections are necessary, at human and technology levels, the more difficult is to outsource. Another impediment is the fact that there is typically little understanding of the existent service boundaries, requirements, costs and profitability. As such decisions are the result of "intuition".

Outsourcing exists at business process level (BPO), IT application level (SaaS), infrastructure (data centre), function or department level (helpdesk, call centre), or combined under a managed services agreement. In general, it is employed when specialized skills are required and it is not your core function.

You already outsource development to contractors, maintenance of the mainframe to suppliers, business strategy development to management consultancies, IT support to specialized IT firms, call centres to India, payroll to China, HR to specialized agencies and so on.

Enterprise Modelling would prepare the ground for outsourcing by showing all parameters of a Function starting with the process, technology and people belonging to it, the costs and KPIs associated to it etc. The Lines would describe the interface to other business functions. The EA framework would support a rapid transition to outsourcing at all layers: Process, Application, Infrastructure and People.

The Operations, Support and Development functions may all be outsourced depending on your business model. That is, the way you decided to make money would stress specific links of your Value Chain, leaving out others which can be outsourced.

Framework for Security Architecture

Enterprise security architecture is, in actual fact, about controlling and protecting access to the Enterprise assets. For that, a strong concept is the "perimeter". We surround an asset, or a group of assets, with a perimeter at which we install protective measures. Then we have to secure the communications and transports between secure perimeters.

The logical security architecture begins at the business level by discovering the existing assets of information, processes, business strategy, planning... to which access needs to be managed.

The next step is to devise the type of access (Read, Write, Update...) for each role, and an Access Control List (ACL) for the asset. People and systems would be assigned roles.

The access type: it can be physical or remote, over networks particularly with regard to IT.

At the Business Layer, an Actor would be assigned a role and specific rights with regard to business artefacts and process execution.

At the Applications Layer, these rights would materialize in Access rights to content, structured data and application (right to reverse an EFTPOS transaction, for instance).

At the infrastructure layer, the rights to manage platforms, OSs, servers, storage and networks would also have to be controlled by similar mechanisms. Actors are assigned roles with standard rights to infrastructure assets.

The Enterprise assets, become components of the Security Architecture; they should already be objects in the EA and its repository, having a description and access rights for various roles. Assets belong to business Functions. Right clicking on an object may pop up a security rights screen.

At the technology layer, access rights to non-IT assets (paper documents, equipment...) but equally EA objects, must be established. Security must be also enforced for real estate and facilities with access controlled at the perimeter around workplaces, especially at gates, doors and cabinets inside buildings.

Nevertheless, before costly security systems are put in place (such as video cameras, 128bit encryption etc.), a threat and risk analysis would be performed to learn how often and how damaging could a threat be. Once the potential loss analyzed, an estimate of the worth of the security method and system could be produced.

At the people layer, security access cards and remote access authentication tokens could be provided besides passwords.

For remote access, VPNs or SSL with encryption for information integrity and confidentiality should be utilized. Measures should be put in place to detect Denial of Service attacks and Man in the Middles message modification.

In summary, every component of every EA layer should be analyzed from a security standpoint and accordingly protected, given the level of threat and potential damage to the Enterprise.

Framework for a Start-Up Business

How would a Small or Medium Business (SMB) adopt EA? A simplified framework can be used as a guideline for entrepreneurs to plan and build the new company. The EA framework already contains the main aspects an entrepreneur needs to consider:

.a. determine the business architecture layer first

- o the product, the business mission
- o the vision, business strategy and plan (how to get there), forecasts
- o Value Chain and business model (what markets, customer segments, pricing, costing, core capabilities etc) to serve the mission
- o typical stakeholders: partners, suppliers, financial institutions

.b. define Governance, type of ownership such as Sole Trader, Partnership … and decision making: the managing team roles and responsibilities

.c. specify GODS functions in terms of activities and required resources such as people and technology and estimate costs for each and every function

- o Operations: sales, services, inbound/outbound logistics, distribution channels, manufacturing
- o Development (R&D, product and capability development) functions
- o Support functions ; decide their business model (how do they produce value to the company) and outsource if necessary

.d. select basic technology for each function, deploy an ERP, use managed services...

.e. sketch key aspects: locations, data, security, planning, required performance (from benchmarking data)

.f. Produce the business plan including all the above.

ANNEX 4. USEFUL ENTERPRISE MODELLING ARTEFACTS

How to design your Processes around the customer

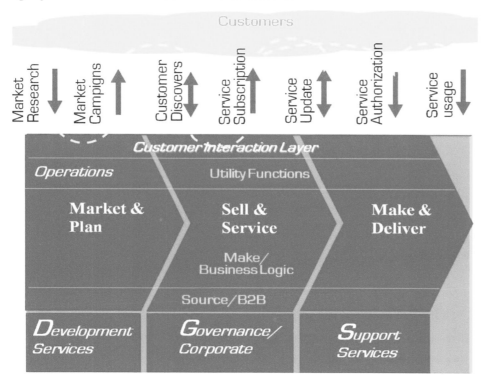

Some of the following business activities have to be strengthened up to transform your organization into a customer centric one.

- Market research (customer needs, trends, competitors' products) resulting in customer segmentation, new product concepts.
- Market campaigns based on research to attract prospects
- Customer interaction at the Portal, Shops, Call Centres...
- The Booking/Reservation/Subscription/Application for Product
- Customer Service and Relationship Management for customer interaction history, personalization, product changes, incentives, loyalty
- Service Authorization and Access
- Service usage (downloading, therapy, access to show, transport...)

The Business (Functions) Reference Map allows a good modelling of the customer interaction.

Enterprise Information Management and Architecture

The typical status of enterprise data

- o Redundant
- o Outdated
- o Corrupted
- o Formatted differently
- o Difficult to find, not readily available in need
- o Silo-ed data repositories, not shared across business

Legitimate queations about data

- o Where do I store or where is the Information?
- o Is this the latest version of the data/document?
- o How can I protect it while ensuring wide access?
- o Who are the Information owners or stewards?
- o How to manage records?
- o Is there a big picture of all Information in the enterprise?
- o For how long are we keeping the data?
- o What should I use: Outlook, SharePoint, shared drive...?

Data must be

- o cleaned
- o structured
- o normalised
- o protected
- o documented
- o archived
- o returned on demand (Freedom of Information)

Legal and regulatory drivers to comply with

- o Respond to FOI (Freedom of Information) requests
- o Secure sensitive Information under the Data Protection Act
- o Provide Records Management , Retention, Archiving strategy

This is the work and purpose of the Enterprise Information Management function with the support of the architecture team. Enterprise Information Management consists of many aspects though as illustrated in the picture.

The Enterprise Information Synoptic View (EIM)

A few definitions and clarifications with regard to Information and data:

- ▪ the Data term is used in a computing context
  - o "Structured" data is found in databases
  - o because it is structured it can be manipulated at record level
- ▪ Information is data in a context addressing a human audience
  - o the data in an invoice, contract, sales report in the context of a document such as word, presentation, spreadsheet
  - o the content in digital media such as video or picture

o can be tagged but the information inside is "unstructured"

This is a tableau of what we have to do to manage our information, content, data... But the Business Intelligence, Data Warehousing, Predictive Analysis, Document and Web Content Management, Master Data Management... are all worth their own are all enterprise Capabilities consisting of functions and applications that should be described in their own views.

An EIM Framework

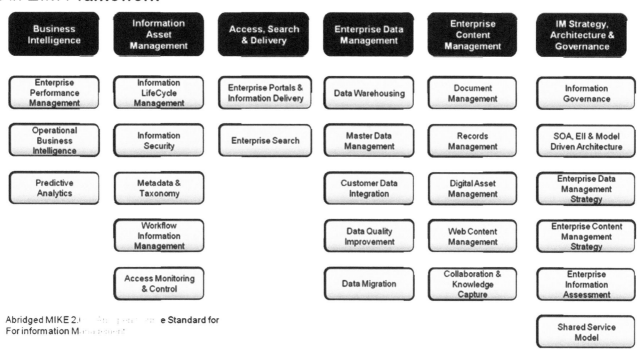

A document is information in reading format.

A Record is a document retained as proof of a transaction, whose content remains frozen for the rest of the lifecycle, once it is marked as such.

An information asset is a unit of information that presents value to a stakeholder, information manipulated as a whole (CRUD: Created, Updated, Deleted) with a single lifecycle.

Create top level Information Register

It should be created to list all key information records, ownership, their access rights, retainment policy...

Information Object	Owner Group	Team	Personal data (DPA)	Confidential class	Access Rights	Review trigger	Retention Period	Archive status
Vendor details	Operations	Finance	N	Unrestricted	All	Review after 6 months	Whilst current	Indefinite
Case Record -	Consumer	Consumer Protection	Y	Confidential	All	2 years post closure	5 years	
Employee record	Operations	HR	Y	Restricted	HR	6 years after leaving	6 years from termination	

Sample top level models for a medical insurance

Stakeholders' use cases

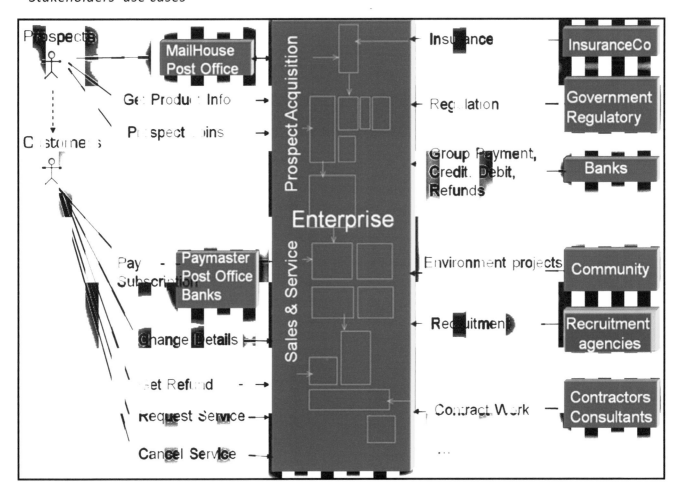

A Health Insurance single page Operations Business Architecture

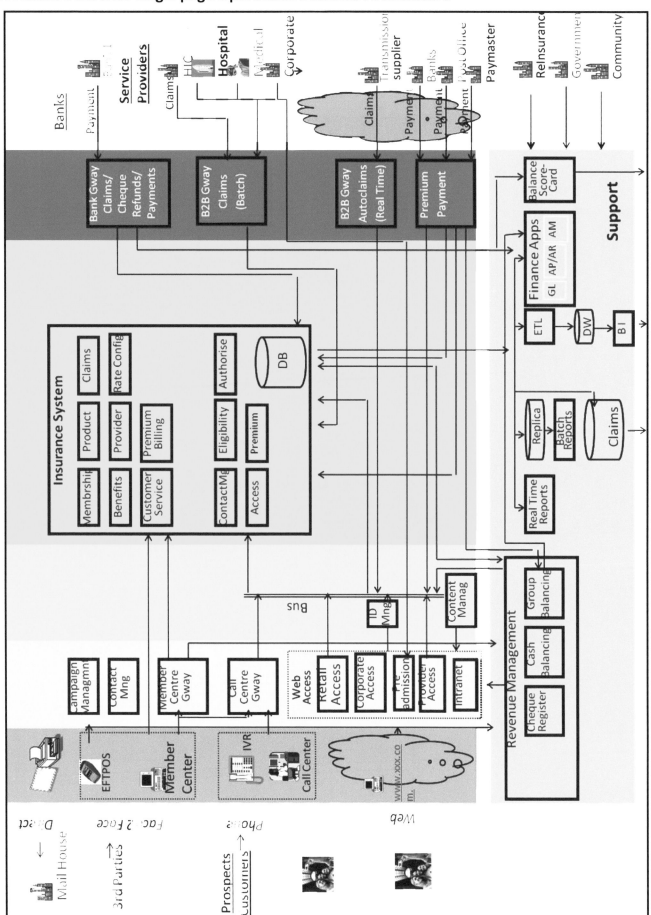

IT Support Applications Functions (Categories) and Applications Map

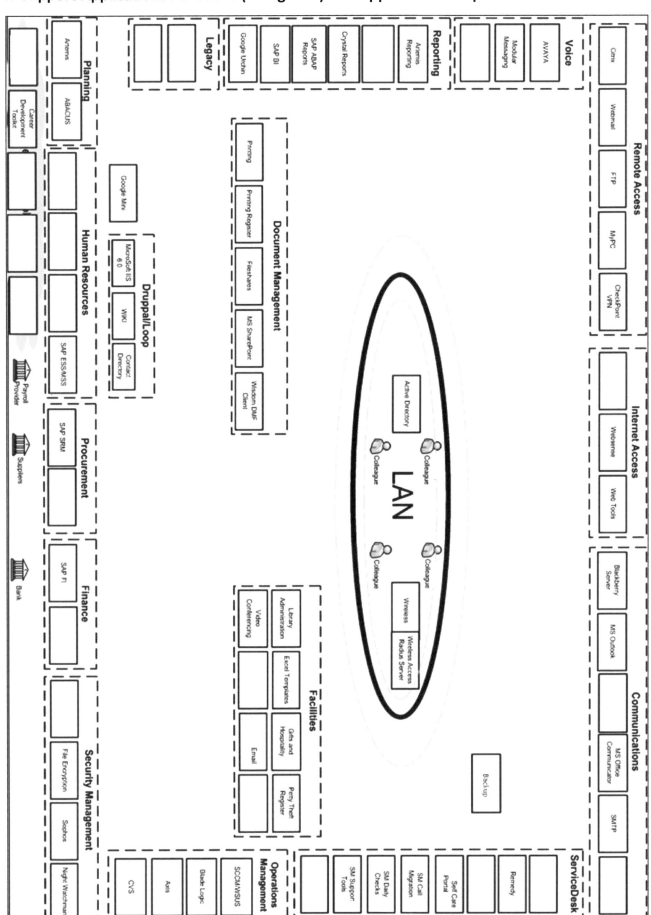

Sample employee Desktop Applications Map

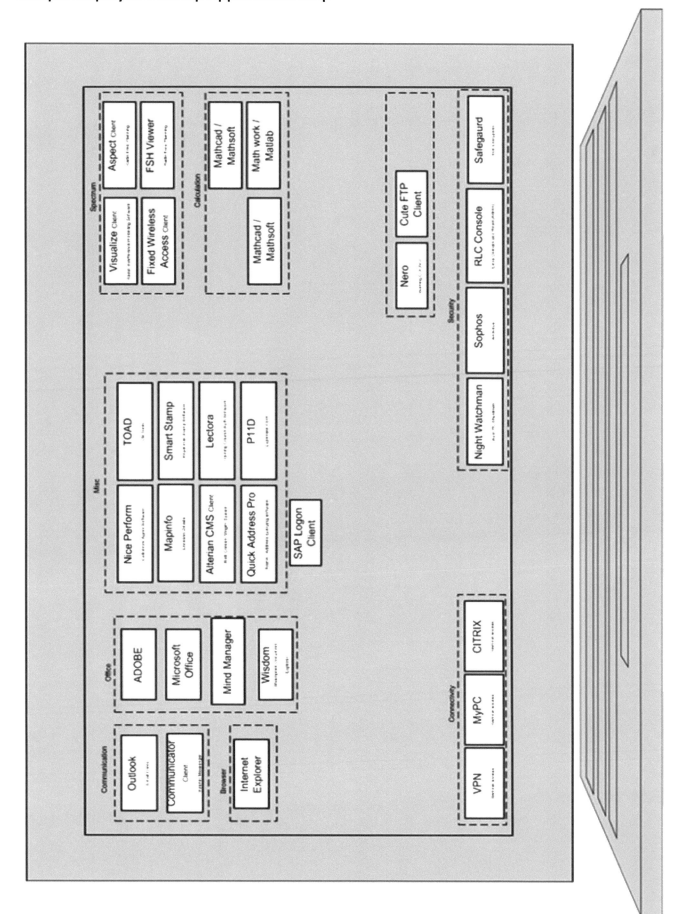

An Enterprise Modelling Framework for Telecoms Architecture Navigation

System Views

Telecom Views
- *Net Elem View*
- Traffic View
- Control View
- Location View
- Presence View
- LI View
- Availability View
- BC/DR View
- Data View

Transport Views
- TCP/UDP
- HTTP
- IP View
- ATM View
- MPLS View
- VPN Views

Transmission Views
- Optical
- SDH
- PDH
- Dark Fiber
- Electrical
- E1
- Giga Ethernet

Protocol Views
- 2G Access
- 3G Access
- CS Core
- PS Core

IT/View

Horizontal View
- Provisioning
- Billing
- Customer Care

Zachman

WHWWWWW
- *What*
- How
- Where
- Who
- When
- Why

Decomposition
- Context
- *Business*
  - Logical
    - 1 Domain
    - 2 BE
    - 3 Data/Obj
  - Implemetatior
  - Detail

The Telecoms Service Delivery Platform Business Map

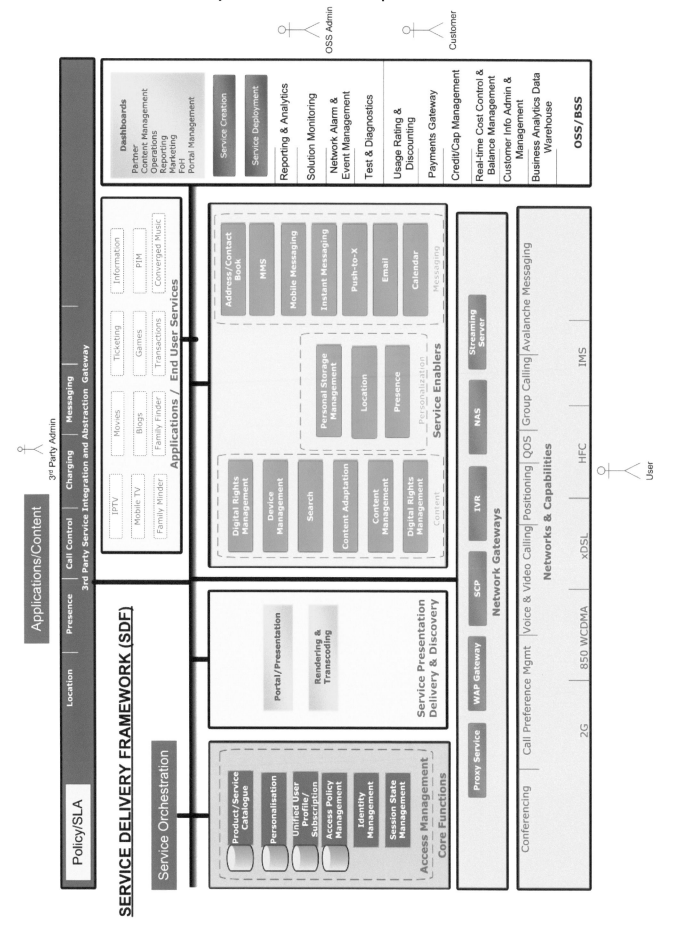

ANNEX 5. BUSINESS DESIGN APPROACHES

Value Chains versus Business Models

Value Chains (VC)

In the 1980s, Michael Porter proposed the Value Chain (VC) concept to illustrate the operation of a company. The business logic of the company is often expressed today as a Value Chain.

A Value Chain is a set of activities that an organization carries out to deliver value to its customers and return a margin of profit to the company and stakeholders.

The profit is the VC margin, as in Porter's picture.

Revenue returned - Costs = Profit Margin

Business Models (BM)

On the other hand, a Business Model (BM) shows the way a company, in delivering to its customers, makes profit and, in general, returns value to its stakeholders.

Osterwalder Business Models

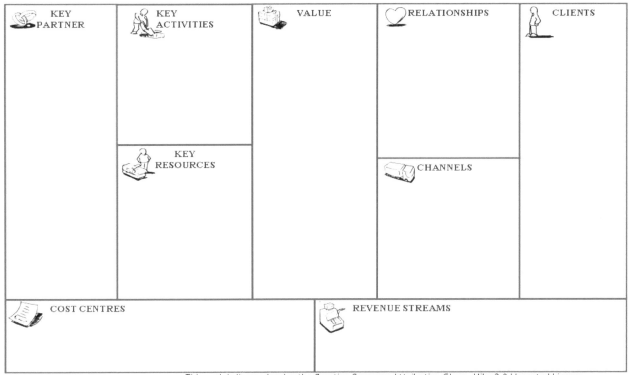

The major elements that determine a Business Model were defined as

- customer Segments
- channels employed to reach customers
- specific types of Customer Relationships
- key Activities - the processes involved in manufacturing and delivering the product
- key Resources - the physical resources that execute the key activities
- kind of Partnerships with 3rd parties that execute activities and provide key deliverables
- Revenue Streams - the revenue generated by this Business Model
- Costs - per activities and resources.

Ultimately, the Value Proposition financially quantifies the worth of the Business Model.

Here is Osterwalder's and Pigneur's BM canvas.

Some enterprises choose to deliver luxury products while manufacturing takes place inhouse. Some chose to sell online bottom priced products. Both companies make profit though, but in different ways. Hence, the Business Model, is the specific enterprise configuration that makes it profitable, generally speaking.

Because it works back from the profit realised or desired, to discover how it is made by looking at customer segments and delivery channels, manufacturing processes and physical resources and partnerships, the

Business Model analyses as such the activities and costs of the Value Chain that delivers the product and returns profit.

Value Chains versus Business Models

While a Business Model (BM) identifies the way a company (activities, resources, channels, partnerships... as described in the BM canvas) returns value/profit while delivering the product, the Value Chain identifies the company sequence of activities (from sourcing to marketing and sales) that deliver the product while returning a "Margin" to the company.

While the Business Model evaluates the returns to the company in terms of Value Proposition, Porter's concept of "Margin" quantifies the profitability of the Value Chain in financial terms only.

The BM primarily stresses the returns of the company approach to product delivery, the VC first identifies the key activities that add value in the process.

But there is always a Value Chain that implements a Business Model. As a corollary, any Business Model should be evaluated or built on the Value Chain that realises it.

The Value Chain is the business concept that enables the Business Model assessment.

The Value Chain a Business Model is evaluated upon, would identify the key sequence of activities that deliver the product. Based on these, the associated resources and partnerships can be analysed to determine the Value Proposition.

Therefore, in addition to representing a Business Model as a number of boxes on a canvas, you can represent it as the associated Value Chain that returns a Margin to the business.

Here is a mapping between the generic Business Model and Value Chain representation.

The Business Model Partners would be mapped all along the Value Chain Inbound Logistics, Operations...

The BM key Activities would be the Porter's VC Primary activities while the BM Channels would be part of the VC Sales and Services.

The Value Chain becomes as such the basis for analysis and construction of a Business Model.

The Business Model would also distinguish the key elements of the Value Chain that differentiate the company.

In brief, a business model describes a configuration of the enterprise architecture, that is, of the processes and the organizational and technology resources implementing them. This configuration delivers the products to specific customer segments through selected channels and returns revenue and costs, as evaluated in the business model. Partnerships and relationships are important for the BM because they can reflect either outsourcing of activities to partners for example or loyalty discounts for customers that reflect in costs.

To estimate the costs and revenue for the calculation of profitability, the BM value chain should be mapped though on the enterprise architecture that exhibits of the processes and the resources that deliver the product deliver value and return profit. In fact, the Enterprise Architecture should be developed in the first place starting from the Value Chain.

A Business Model may be represented as such, as a path through an Enterprise Model or Enterprise wide Architecture, that illustrates the customer segments, channels, activities, the resources that execute them.

The Business Model elements of Value Proposition and Cost Structure are part financial calculations rather than constituting components of an architecture.

Design Thinking

Still, business process re-design as such is not really the object of Enterprise Modelling, but often a business goal to humanize the User Experience (UX).

Hence, Design Thinking addresses business processes improvement rather than the method to model the enterprise. Design Thinking (DT) proposes a straightforward human experience in interacting with an enterprise. It acts to simplify processes, to design natural user interfaces (UIs) and adapt them to access terminals...

The design of the interaction with the customer has to have in mind the audience, its age, education, degree of (dis-)ability... Digital appliances are often abandoned because people cannot remember to press three times a button to change a setting. Few check the instructions today. Interfaces have to come naturally, self explanatory based on our good common experiences. UI used to be and is a differentiator in selecting a mobile phone.

Design Thinking (DT) can make a difference in adopting an application such as Sales or Customer Relationship Management. It makes a difference in selecting a service provider. It maybe be applied to services for any internal or external stakeholders to make their work more productive, error free and more profitable for the company. Since DT ends up changing the enterprise processes, technology, UIs..., the transformation should be performed and documented under the Enterprise Modelling effort. But EM and EA also have a role in managing the inner complexity of an enterprise to reduce duplication and unnecessary variations while enforcing modularisation, standardisation.

But, ultimately, DT and EM, EA are different disciplines that are performed by different teams. While one focuses on streamlining the human experience in the enterprise, the other on optimising the enterprise by discovering, documenting and structuring the enterprise.

DT maybe a tool though in the EM?EA arsenal that comes with a set of methods and principles. Design Thinking has not the same meaning as enterprise or business design. It is only a part of it. Enterprise or Business Design denote designing and implementing the enterprise starting with a blueprint.

Service Blueprinting

Check the Learning Space Toolkit,

http://learningspacetoolkit.org/services-and-support/service-design-process/

ServicePlotTM for understanding your service philosophy, values, and vision

Personas Overview to depict the motivations and behaviours of your users

Service Location Planner to determine what services will be offered where, when, and by whom

Customer Journey Map to plot the use of a service/space overtime and identify the moments of interaction or "touchpoints" Service Blueprints to provide guidance on how both front-line staff and those behind-the-scenes will provide a service through different channels"

"A service blueprint is an operational planning tool that provides guidance on how a service will be provided, specifying the physical evidence, staff actions, and support systems / infrastructure needed to deliver the service across its different channels". (Wikipedia).

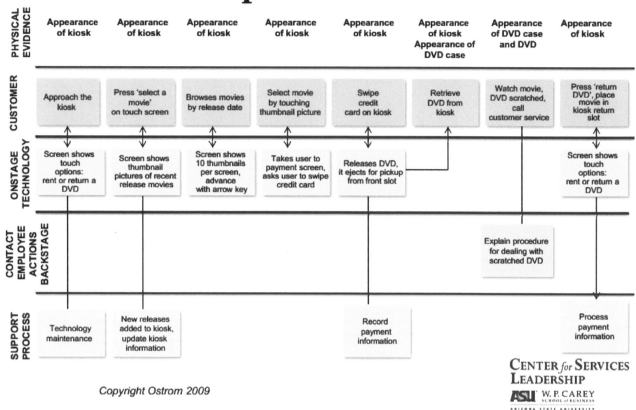

THE AUTHOR

Adrian is an executive level consultant in enterprise modelling/architecture. He used to head the enterprise architecture function at Ofcom UK, and used to be the Chief Architect for the TM Forum Frameworx. He worked as a high technology, enterprise architecture and strategy senior manager for Accenture, Vodafone and Nokia, and as a principal consultant and lead architect at Qantas, Logica, Lucent Bell Labs...

He is the author of a few books on Enterprise Architecture modelling and development, and published numerous articles and had two blogs, summed up in two books now.

REFERENCES

a) EA slideshow: Enterprise Architecture in 3minutes or so

http://www.slideshare.net/Grigoriu/enterprise-architecture-in-3-minutes-or-so-v1

b) Blogs http://it.toolbox.com/blogs/ea-matters

c) EA books: http://www.amazon.com/Adrian-Grigoriu/e/B007NGB1XY

d) An Enterprise Architecture Development Framework, Kindle, 4th edition

https://www.amazon.com/Enterprise-Architecture-Development-Framework-4th-ebook/dp/B004JN0KYA?ie=UTF8&ref_=asap_bc

e) Book "An Enterprise Architecture Development Framework" from Trafford...

http://www.trafford.com/Bookstore/BookDetail.aspx?Book=179897

f) The Enterprise Architecture Matters blog

https://www.amazon.com/Enterprise-Architecture-matters-blog-ebook/dp/B00C3MJJ1O?ie=UTF8&ref_=asap_bc

g) EA site: http://www.enterprise-architecture-matters.co.uk

h) Presentations: https://www.youtube.com/user/MrGrigoriu

http://www.authorstream.com/grigoriu/

i) The GODS one page generic Business Architecture

https://www.youtube.com/watch?v=yYP9RpVTLXA

j) Enterprise Architecture roadblocks and remedies

http://www.authorstream.com/Presentation/grigoriu-1631385-enterprise-architecture-roadblocks-remedies/

k) Papers: http://www.bptrends.com/?s=grigoriu

l) Paper: A single Page generic Business Architecture

http://www.bptrends.com/bpt/wp-content/publicationfiles/FOUR%2012-07-10-ART-A%20Single%20Page%20Generic%20BA-Grigoriu.pdf

m) Paper: The Virtualisation of the Enterprise

http://www.bptrends.com/bpt/wp-content/publicationfiles/04-08-ART-THREE-TheVirtualizationoftheEnterprise-Grigoriu-JE-V._2_.doc.pdf

n) Paper: The Cloud Enterprise

http://www.bptrends.com/bpt/wp-content/publicationfiles/TWO_04-09-ART-The_Cloud_Enterprise-Grigoriu_v1-final.pdf

o)   The Academy Papers

https://independent.academia.edu/AdrianGrigoriu

p) Paper: A Comparison of Business Process Modelling approaches

https://www.bptrends.com/bpt/wp-content/publicationfiles/03%2D11%2D2011%2DART%2DComparion%20of%20business%20modelling%20approaches%20to%20GODS%2DGrigoriu%2Dph%2Epdf

THE ENTERPRISE MODELLING POSTERS

The overall enterprise modelling is summarised in a few key sections and A3 posters, attached.

System Modelling 101

Explains the system modelling framework, sequence and diagram types.

Describes the enterprise FFLV framework as a three dimensional body which dimensions are the Functions (Nodes), Flows (Signals) and resource Layers.

Any model would consist of these three dimensions (Functions in Flows in a Layer) and would be situated accordingly in the body of the 3D system.

The modelling is done by comparison to human body description by anatomy and physiology. The modelling sequence consists in the identification of stakeholders, Use Cases and related Capabilities, the Flows (Signals) and the Functions Nodes), interfaces, links...

The section (and associated poster) is a prerequisite to the Enterprise Modelling process since the Enterprise is a complex System.

The Framework: the Enterprise Modelling Framework and Metamodel

The modelling framework, FFLV, defines the key dimensions of the Enterprise Model 3D representation.

In addition to dimensions, the metamodel illustrates the other parameters of the model dimensions (information, interfaces, rules) and their relationships.

Any blueprint should consist of components of the type exposed in the metamodel, in the specified relationships.

The framework recommends an one page generic enterprise business architecture, GODS, consisting of a generic Value Chain and supporting capabilities. GODS is a blueprint illustrating the key Capabilities as Flows over the Functions of a generic enterprise.

An extended framework also recommends architecture and design principles that shape a technically correct architecture against which the architecture debt is measured.

The Modelling Framework should be adopted and embedded in your enterprise modelling approach and tool.

The framework representation must be embedded in the modelling tool as a Graphical User Interface for access and navigation across the EM artefacts and their components, links, flows, interfaces and information. The metamodel should be reflected in the EM component repository schema to determine the implicit component types and their connections.

The Models: the Reference Models and Modelling Sequence

Provides the enterprise modeller with typical generic models and diagrams to jump start the development. There is no point to start from scratch each and every effort.

The chapter and poster supplies the templates and a design sequence that begins with the Stakeholders' Use Cases, continues with the Functions block diagram (constituting a Business Reference Map), Business Flow maps, high level generic Information, Applications and Infrastructure Maps and ends with the People organisation chart alignment.

Use it for the Design sequence and high level templates all mapped on the Business Functions Reference Map or Capability Map.

The Design: the Enterprise Model Integrated Design

The Design illustrates the synoptic Enterprise Model as a set of architecture blueprints which components and relationships are prescripted in the metamodel.

In this poster and section, the Enterprise Model is represented as an interconnected set of template models of the types described in the reference models and modelling sequence section.

Use this section to understand the linkage between the enterprise key blueprints that form Enterprise Model.

While the Design blueprint illustrates a high level generic model of an enterprise, each and every blueprint can be further decomposed to further levels of detail. New aspects of the enterprise can be added at any time to this model both in the business and resources layers.

The Process: the Modelling and Transformation process

showing the key stages of enterprise modelling and transformation, key activities and deliverables at each step, the modelling organisation and governance, the good practices for site, governance, team organisation and the tools to measure progress maturity, value created and evaluate the EA business case.

The Strategy: Design and Mapping

The end to end strategy design framework and process starting from the environment and market trends and stakeholders' needs, strengths and weaknesses, current strategy... to the mapping to the enterprise capabilities and roadmapping them to execute the enterprise transformation.

Use this section and poster to devise the enterprise strategy from scratch from external and internal factors, realise Vision and map the strategy to business capabilities and units and ultimately down to the IT capabilities that implement the functionality of the enterprise.

The Enterprise Model

shows how the key models fit into the Enterprise Model cube side by side. Used as a simple recap picture.

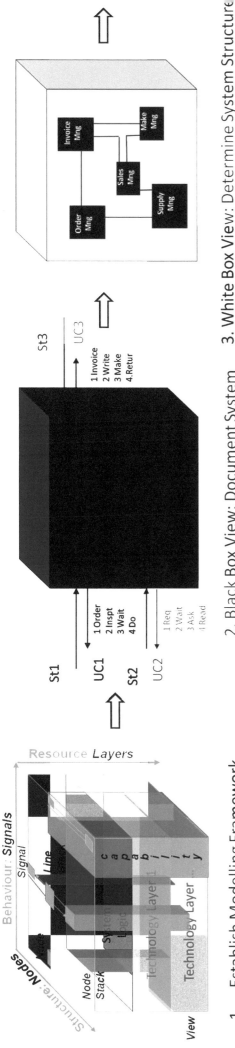

1. Establish Modelling Framework

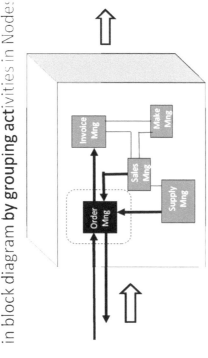

2. Black Box View: Document System Context and Use Case **Scenarios**

3. White Box View: Determine System Structure in block diagram **by grouping activities in Nodes**

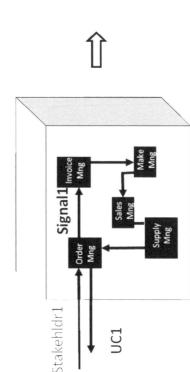

4. Model dynamic behaviour/operation for each scenario in Signals over **Nodes Swimlane**/Object/Sequence diagrams

5. **Illustrate State Transitions on Messages** /Events for each **Function, if stateful**

6. Identify perm Links and Interfaces by **analysing every Node I/O**

7. Identify in **each Node the** Data, decision points **and Rules for branching**

8. Identify physical technology architecture layers, their nodes and links **and apply flows**

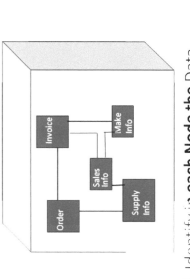

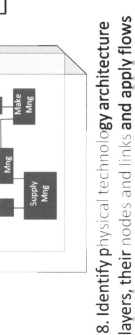

9. Key System Modelling diagrams

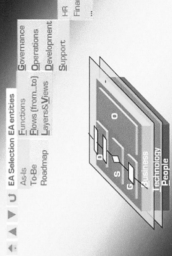

Simple modular metamodel

(Business Structure: Functions — Business Operation: Flows — Applications — Technology — Infrastructure — People — Information)

Modular Metamodel

People · Technology · Business

- Organisation Architecture
- Infrastructure Architecture
- Applications Architecture
- Non-IT Technology Architecture
- Business Flows
- Business Functions Map
- Context View

Capability/Service/Solution Architect. components models

Navigation of the enterprise model

EA Selection EA entities
- As-Is · Functions · Governance
- To-Be · Flows (from..to) · Operations
- Roadmap · Layers&Views · Development
- Support

HR · Finance

Business · Technology · People

Implementation Resource: Layers

Operation: Flows — Visualisation: Views — Structure: Functions

Process stack · Function stack · Link Stack · Service Stack · Sublayers

Business Logic · Technology · People · Applications · Servers and Storage · Networks · Resources · Cap 1 · Cap n

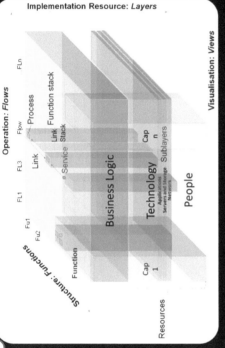

The enterprise modelled as a three dimensional body

	Nodes	Lines	Nodes
Business	Process	Flow	Process
Applications	Service	Req/Resp (ESB, WS SOAP/XML, REST)	Service
	Application (ERP, CRM...)	Information Exchange/EAI, CORBA	Application
Infrastructure		DAS, NAS, SAN	DAS, NAS, SAN
Storage	SW side: Application, DB, Web...	(i)SCSI, Fibre Channel (FC)	
Servers	HW side	JMS, MQ...	HW Serv
		Sockets: UDP, TCP/IP protocols	Gateways, DNS
Networks	Switch, Routers	MPLS, ATM, FR, Copper	Hubs, Bridges
WAN	Hubs, Bridges	Ethernet	Hubs, Bridges
LAN			

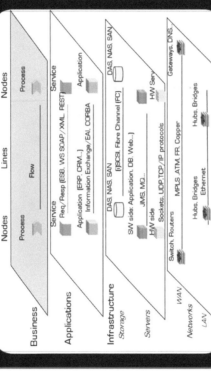

Nodes and Lines patterns in model layers

Functions · Flows · Layers · Views

Development D · Governance G · Support S · Operations O · Outcomes/Lines

Business · Technology · People

The FFLV-GODS enterprise modelling framework

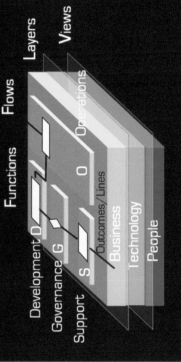

An Enterprise consists of a group of people organised to deliver a product employing technology.

The Enterprise Model (EM) is a graphical description of the enterprise that consists of a navigable set of integrated diagrams.
As opposed to Enterprise Architecture (EA), the Enterprise Model covers, beside IT, the enterprise Business Logic, People Organisation and non-IT technology.
An enterprise can be modelled in three dimensions as Structure (Nodes/Functions+Links) Operation (Signals/Flows), Implementation Resource in Layers, visualised in Views, filtering only the enterprise aspects of interest.

The Enterprise Modelling Framework is a frame on which the artefacts, modelled independently, mount to give the whole EM. All artefacts consist of one or more framework components/dimensions.
Modelling principles are part of the framework.
A metamodel is an entity relationship diagram illustrating the component and relationships types of the Enterprise Model.

Why Enterprise Modelling?
Enterprise Modelling enables enterprise understanding, problem solving, improvement, simplification, integration, investment, decision making..., resources alignment to intended business operation... strategy mapping to EM for execution.
Overall, EM is an enterprise reusable asset that, over time, facilitates:
- enhanced management of enterprise complexity
- faster enterprise change and transformation, that is agility to market changes

Who does EM?
The Enterprise Modeller in Chief and team
- specific the EM framework, standards, principles, guidelines...
- organise and coordinates the EM work so that stakeholders' parts fit consistently into the framework and enterprise model.
- design the one page enterprise models
Stakeholders model and document the views of aspects they own.
Enterprise Modelling is an enterprise wide effort.

FFLV framework elements: Functions (Nodes), Flows (Signals), Layers, Views.
Functions: clusters of related functionality, logical blocks in which the Enterprise is structured. A Function consists of Processes, Information, Rules and Interfaces.
Function Stack: Functions + executing Technology + People roles
A Flow: an end to end sequence of processes, that deliver an outcome.
A Process is an activity and key element of both Functions and Flows.
Information is stored & processed in Functions and transmitted in Flows.
Information is implemented as data in the Technology layer.
A Capability: an operation the enterprise can perform that consists in Functions, Flows and related People & Technology that execute them. An enterprise is said to have capabilities. Employed in strategy mapping and enterprise comparisons.
A Service: an encapsulated capability accessed through an interface.
Views are filters excluding all but the enterprise aspect of concern to a stakeholder, represented as cross-sections through the Enterprise body.

GODS – Governance, Operations, Development, Support
the basic Functions of any Enterprise.

Architecture Principles
Decoupling, Modularization, Encapsulation, Layering, Hierarchical design, Distribution agnostic, Standardization, Duplication reduction
Design Guidelines: design SOA, Virtualise technology, Use technology Appliances, Converge data, voice and video networks, Lease/Buy/Build.

EM outcomes
- The integrated business logic, organization and technology blueprints for the current and target Enterprise states.
- The framework, principles, standards, best practices...
- The transition roadmap from current to targets

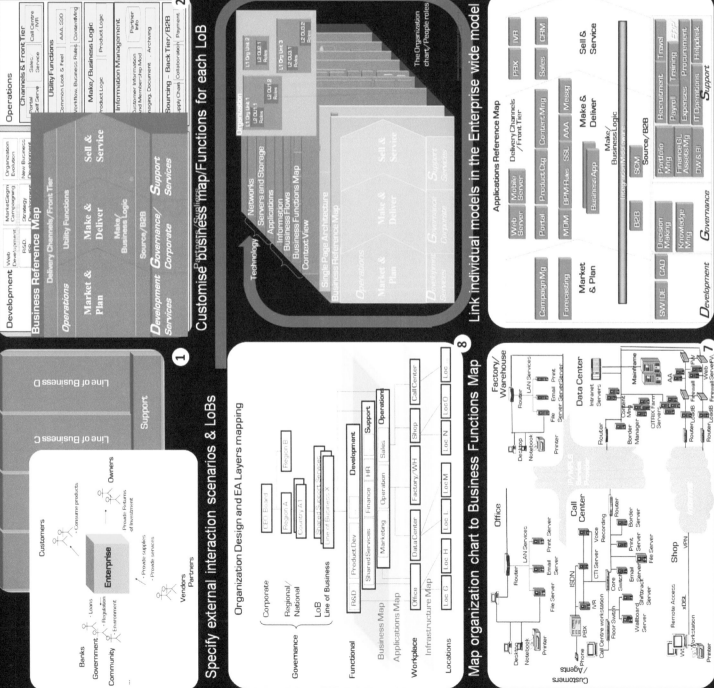

1 Specify external interaction scenarios & LoBs

2 Customise business map/Supplier map/Functions for each LoB

Business Reference Map

3 Design key flows and business architecture

4 Document key Flows. Use this business map

5 Specify Information Model on Business Map

6 Design Applications Model on Business Map

7 Design Infrastructure Model - Servers Storage Networks

8 Map organization chart to Business Functions Map

9 Link individual models in the Enterprise wide model

Organization Design and EA Layers mapping

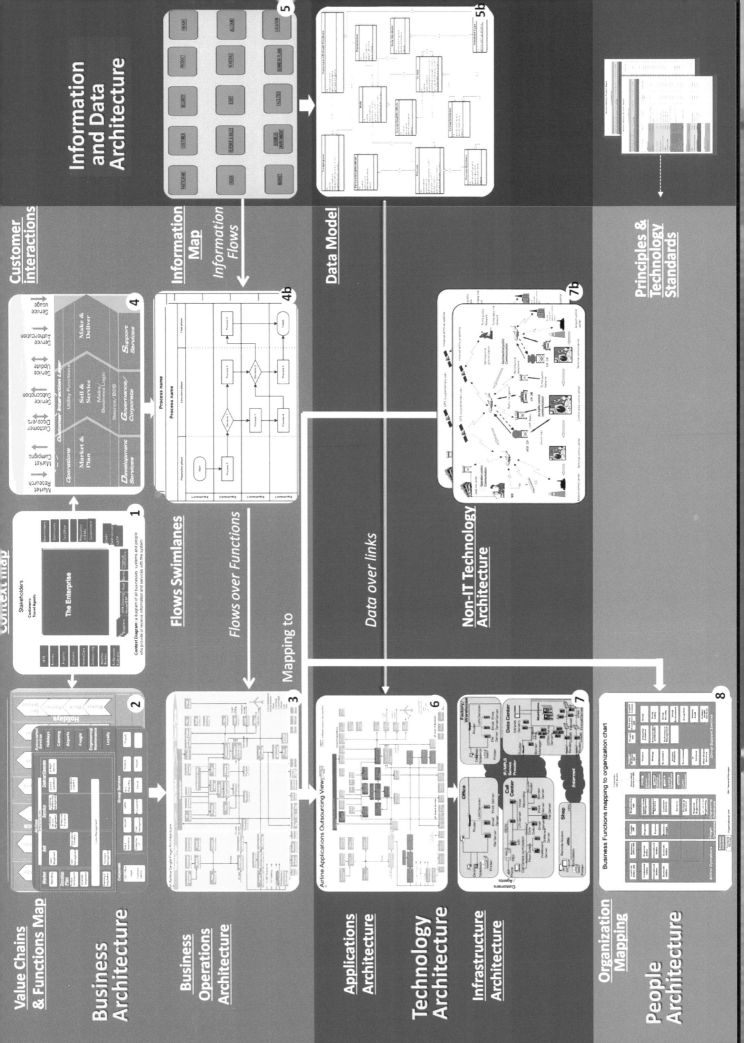

Information and Data Architecture

Customer interactions

Information Map

Information Flows

Data Model

5

5b

Principles & Technology Standards

Value Chains & Functions Map

Business Architecture

1

2

Business Operations Architecture

Flows Swimlanes

Flows over Functions

4

4b

3

Mapping to

Data over links

Non-IT Technology Architecture

7b

Applications Architecture

Technology Architecture

Infrastructure Architecture

6

7

Organization Mapping

People Architecture

8

Set-up

EM maybe triggered by
1. An imminent Merger or Acquisition (M&A)
2. A decision to outsource business functions
3. Adoption of Cloud strategy
4. A requirement to implement regulatory changes
5. A business process improvement initiative
6. A company re-organization
7. Adoption of new business models
8. An upgrade of obsolete key technology
9. Establishment of a new company
10. Conscient decision to better the enterprise

The EA Set-up Activities
1. Define enterprise modelling, outcome, scope
2. Do Business Case and get approval
3. Specify practice organization and governance
4. Propose the first 100 days development plan
5. Define modeling framework, metamodel, principles
6. Establish modelling process best practices
7. Select EM tool, embed framework, organise site
8. Capture information on existing organization, products, stakeholders, strategy, objectives, business and operating models, roadmapping...

The process of building the EM is iterative, going into further depths and new entities and views are added.

As-Is Modelling

1. Produce value proposition for specific iteration
2. Devise As-Is Business Functions (Reference) Map
3. Specify stakeholders' Use Cases and Capabilities
4. Document a business flows map and model flows over functions in swimlane/sequence charts
5. Model As-Is Single Page Business Architecture using templates as flows over key functions&links
6. For each Function identify technology/people roles over business functions
7. Map Information onto Business functions
8. Map applications against business functions
9. Map IT data architecture against functions map
10. Do non-IT technology architecture for function map
11. Draw Infrastructure architecture: servers, storage, networks
12. Do organization chart and map to business functions map
13. Design Enterprise wide views over the functions map : Security, Location, Performance, Financials...
14. Asses and map enterprise capabilities to key functions and flows
15. Iterate designing capability by capability

Do Top-down business discovery employing framework templates and Bottom-Up design of existing technology

To-Be Design & Planning

Design target Capabilities views as Business Functions and Flows Map, Applications, Infrastructure and non-IT technology architectures
1. Compile apps & technology obsolescence roadmap
2. Map strategy to Enterprise Capabilities and subsequently to their Functions, Flows, Organisation and Technology
3. Design the enterprise To-Be business functions and capabilities map
4. Documented target business flows starting with the customer facing functions and products
5. Model the target Single Page Architecture as key Flows over Functions
6. Update current Information Architecture (IA)
7. Update current Data Architecture and map to IA
8. Draft SOA like business services
9. Draw target infrastructure blueprints servers, storage and networks diagrams, cloud, inventory
10. Do target people organisation
11. Do Gap analysis
12. Produce Enterprise Transformation roadmap
13. Do Planning of next few EM iterations

Design SOA services that wrap capabilities
Apply Architecture and Design Principles

Transformation

EM assists the cross-functional transformation team to
1. Devise Transformation Program Portfolio from roadmap
   • Implementing in iterations with often deliveries and stakeholders' consultation (Agile)
   • Prioritising to deliver the urgent fixes for the Enterprise
   • Leveraging existing applications and infrastructure
   • Setting value propositions and SMART Deliverables and CSFs, KPIs mission and scope at each iteration
   • Considering dependencies and synchronizations
2. Establish the EM implementation governance
   • Embed EM controls in development processes
3. Execute iteration
   • Re-engineer existing processes and technology
   • Implement new processes, technology, governance
   • Involve outsourcing, managed services companies
   • Work with Suppliers to package applications as services
   • Continuously manage
     • EA risks and roadblocks
     • Communications
     • Change adoption
4. Evaluate value delivered at each iteration
5. Model new requirements and do design in parallel with implementation and utilisation

Exploitation

Measure the Enterprise Model development progress

1. **Stage 0: Pre-EM**
2. **Stage 1:** Set-up phase; EM programme definition. From approved business case till the EM organization is set up, planning and resources are committed and EM modeller, Steering Committee and governance are agreed. Capabilities for design and execution are committed now. EM framework and tools are established
3. **Stage 2:** EM discovery and design; the As-Is Model is discovered, intermediate stages and To-Be EM sketched.
4. **Stage 3:** Transformation Execution; transformation plan approved, KPIs, CSFs and quick wins are determined; execution in iterations until 80/20% (functionality/effort) achieved and value delivered confirmed.
5. **Stage 4:** exploitation stage, while incremental design/plan/implementation stages in execution.

Measure Enterprise Model utilisation process maturity
1. Level 0: EM ignored
2. Level 1: EM occasional exploitation
3. Level 2: Documented EM exploitation
4. Level 3: Managed, embedded, EM always used in decision making and change processes
5. Level 4: Optimizing EM, on-going EM, design the enterprise based on the EM

Drivers for Business Transformation and actions for IT

Business Drivers// Why,Who, Actions	Customer Satisfaction	Operations Streamlining	Financial Fitness	Strategic Strength	Corporate Social Responsibility Legal
Rationale	Increased Competition, Customer Churn	Point Solutions Patching Tame Organic Growth	Revenue Growth Cost Reduction	Cope with amount of information, rate of change, complexity	Increasing Care for the World around
Stake-holder	Customer	Company	Owner	Employee, All	Community/ Government
Business Actions	Improve Response, Usability, Improve New Products and Markets	Simplify Legacy Business improvement Align organization	Prioritize investment Reduce costs	Establish Competitive Advantage Manage Change Manage Innovation Turn Digital	Manage Community/ Environment Manage Compliance to Regulatory
Resulting IT Priorities	Single Customer View (MDM) Self Service Engagement through On line sales Social Media	Cloud Virtualization of Technology One Voice and Data network	IT strategy alignment Single Version of Truth-DW/BI Real Time Business Intelligence	Manage Agile/SOA Risk Management Emerging Technologies Knowledge Management Information Management	Save the environment (recycling...) Community Involvement Disaster Recovery

Solution development process with EM controls

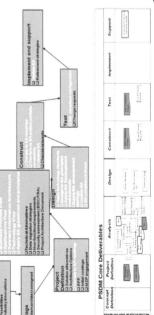

The Business Case, relative to the "No EM" and ROI

Enterprise RoEM = Relative Revenue − Relative Cost

Relative Enterprise Revenue = Rev$_{arch}$ − Rev$_{noarch}$
Increases revenue y% from faster & better products on the market

Relative Costs = Cost$_{arch}$ − Cost$_{noarch}$
Saves z% cost from standardization and rationalization

Making the business case for Enterprise Modelling

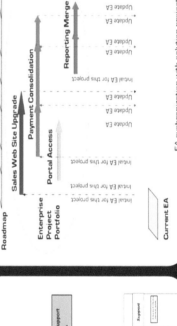

3 Year Roadmap — Enterprise Project Portfolio
Sales Web Site Upgrade — Payment Consolidation — Reporting Merge
Portal Access
Current EA / Target EA — EA sychronization with solution projects

100 days plan for establishing the EM practice

The Enterprise Change/Modelling Cycle and Iterations

Governance checks in capability development process   Solution Architectures alignment to Enterprise Model   The Enterprise Modelling and Transformation Process

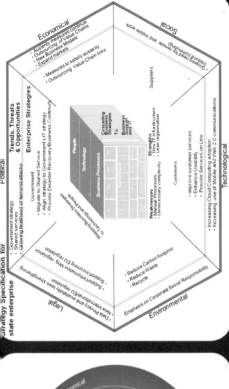

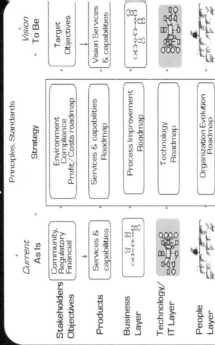

Do environment analysis PESTEL, Poretr's 5fs...

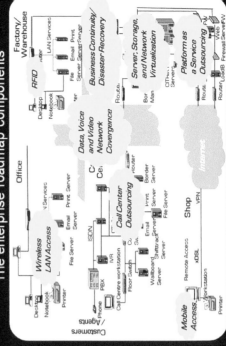

The enterprise roadmap components

Infrastructure goals from strategy mapping

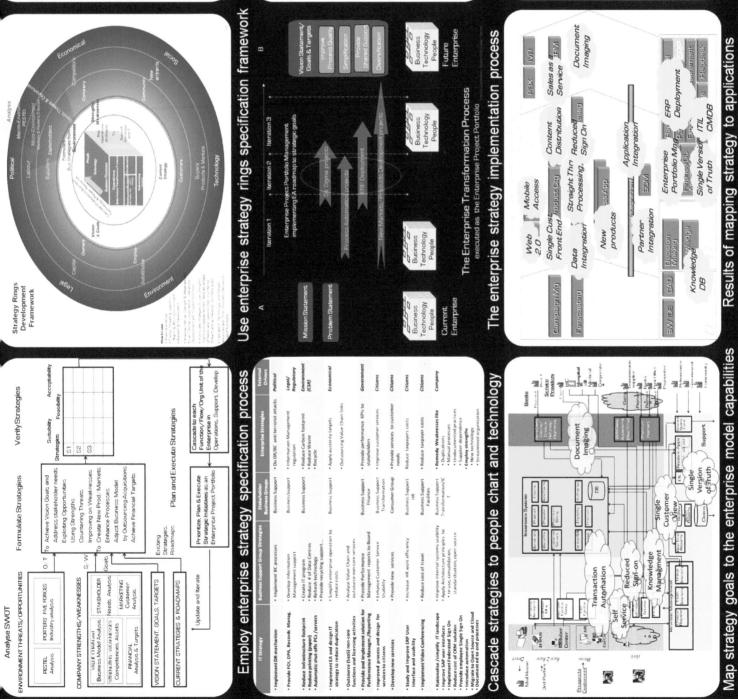

Use enterprise strategy rings specification framework

The enterprise strategy implementation process

Results of mapping strategy to applications

Employ enterprise strategy specification process

Cascade strategies to people chart and technology

Map strategy goals to the enterprise model capabilities

The GOUS-ATLV Enterprise
Modelling Framework

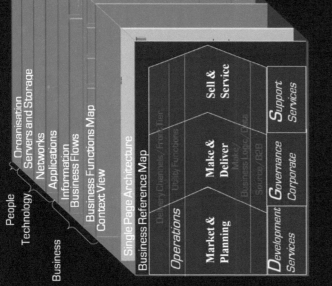

Views

Flows

Layers

Functions

Business

Technology

Context

Functions

Business Architecture

One Page BA

Stakeholders'

Interactions

Flows

Information

Information /DataArchitecture

Data

Applications

Infrastructure

Technology Architecture

Non-IT Technology Architecture

Organisation Architecture

People

Technology

Business

Organisation

Servers and Storage

Networks

Applications

Information

Business Flows

Business Functions Map

Context View

Single Page Architecture

Business Reference Map

Resource

CPSIA information can be obtained
at www.ICGtesting.com
Printed in the USA
BVHW012052120123
656178BV00002B/7